CW00693456

Non-League Football Supporters' Guide & Yearbook 2015

EDITOR
John Robinson

Twenty-third Edition

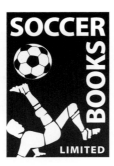

For details of our range of 2,000 books and over 350 DVDs, visit our web site or contact us using the information shown below.

British Library Cataloguing in Publication Data
A catalogue record for this book is available from the British Library

ISBN: 978-1-86223-296-9

Copyright © 2014, SOCCER BOOKS LIMITED (01472 696226)
72 St. Peter's Avenue, Cleethorpes, N.E. Lincolnshire, DN35 8HU, England

Web site   www.soccer-books.co.uk   •   e-mail   info@soccer-books.co.uk

Manufactured in the UK by Ashford Colour Press Ltd.

FOREWORD

Our thanks go to the numerous club officials who have aided us in the compilation of information contained in this guide as well as Michael Robinson (page layouts), Bob Budd (cover artwork) and Tony Brown (Cup Statistics – www.soccerdata.com).

Any readers who have up-to-date ground photographs which they would like us to consider for use in a future edition of this guide are requested to contact us at our address which is shown on the facing page.

The fixtures listed later in this book were released just a short time before we went to print and, as such, some of the dates shown may be subject to change. We therefore suggest that readers treat these fixtures as a rough guide and check dates carefully before attending matches.

Shortly before this publication went to print, Salisbury City FC were expelled from the Conference after failing to meet the terms of membership. The club has stated that they intend to take legal action against the Conference in regards to this expulsion but it does not seem possible that they will be playing in the competition for the 2014/2015 season. Therefore, we have not included a page entry for Salisbury City FC in this guide.

We would like to wish our readers a safe and happy spectating season.

John Robinson
EDITOR

CONTENTS

THE FOOTBALL CONFERENCE NATIONAL

Address   4th Floor, 20 Waterloo Street, Birmingham   B2 5TB

Phone   (0121) 643-3143

Web site   www.footballconference.co.uk

Clubs for the 2014/2015 Season

AFC TELFORD UNITED

Founded: 2004
Former Names: Formed after Telford United FC went out of business. TUFC were previously known as Wellington Town FC
Nickname: 'The Bucks'
Ground: The New Bucks Head Stadium, Watling Street, Wellington, Telford   TF1 2TU
Record Attendance: 13,000 (1935)

Pitch Size: 110 × 74 yards
Colours: White shirts and shorts
Telehone No: (01952) 640064
Fax Number: (01952) 640021
Ground Capacity: 5,780
Seating Capacity: 2,280
Web site: www.telfordunited.com

GENERAL INFORMATION
Car Parking: At the ground
Coach Parking: At the ground
Nearest Railway Station: Wellington
Nearest Bus Station: Wellington
Club Shop: At the ground
Opening Times: Saturday matchdays only from 1.30pm.
Telephone No: None

GROUND INFORMATION
Away Supporters' Entrances & Sections:
Frank Nagington Stand on the rare occasions when segregation is used

ADMISSION INFO (2014/2015 PRICES)
Adult Standing: £13.00
Adult Seating: £13.00
Under-16s Standing: £2.00
Under-16s Seating: £2.00
Under-20s Standing: £5.00
Under-20s Seating: £5.00
Concessionary Standing: £10.00
Concessionary Seating: £10.00

DISABLED INFORMATION
Wheelchairs: Accommodated at both ends of the ground
Helpers: Admitted
Prices: Normal prices apply
Disabled Toilets: Available
Contact: (01952) 640064   (Bookings are not necessary)

Travelling Supporters' Information:
Routes: Exit the M54 at Junction 6 and take the A518. Go straight on at the first roundabout, take the second exit at the next roundabout then turn left at the following roundabout. Follow the road round to the right then turn left into the car park.

ALDERSHOT TOWN FC |

Founded: 2013 (as a new company)
Former Names: Aldershot Town FC
Nickname: 'Shots'
Ground: ESS Stadium, Recreation Ground, High Street, Aldershot GU11 1TW
Record Attendance: 7,500 (18th November 2000)
Pitch Size: 117 × 76 yards

Colours: Red shirts with Blue shorts
Telephone Nº: (01252) 320211
Fax Number: (01252) 324347
Club Secretary: (01252) 320211– Graham Hortop
Ground Capacity: 7,100
Seating Capacity: 1,879
Web site: www.theshots.co.uk
E-mail: enquiries@theshots.co.uk

GENERAL INFORMATION
Supporters Club: c/o Club
Telephone Nº: (01252) 320211
Car Parking: Parsons Barracks Car Park is adjacent
Coach Parking: Contact the club for information
Nearest Railway Station: Aldershot (5 mins. walk)
Nearest Bus Station: Aldershot (5 minutes walk)
Club Shop: At the ground
Opening Times: Saturday matchdays 10.00am to 2.45pm and 9.30am to 7.30pm on Tuesday matchdays.
Telephone Nº: (01252) 320211

GROUND INFORMATION
Away Supporters' Entrances & Sections:
Accommodation in the East Bank Terrace, Bill Warren section (South Stand) – Redan Hill Turnstiles Nº 11 and 12.

ADMISSION INFO (2014/2015 PRICES)
Adult Standing: £17.00
Adult Seating: £19.00
Under-16s Standing: £5.00 (Under-6s admitted free)
Under-16s Seating: £7.00
Concessionary Standing: £13.00
Concessionary Seating: £15.00
Note: Military personnel are charged Concessionary prices
Programme Price: £3.00

DISABLED INFORMATION
Wheelchairs: Accommodated in the North Stand
Helpers: Admitted
Prices: £13.00 for the disabled, free of charge for helpers
Disabled Toilets: Available
Contact: (01252) 320211   (Bookings are required)

Travelling Supporters' Information:
Routes: From the M3: Exit at Junction 4 and follow signs for Aldershot (A331). Leave the A331 at the A323 exit (Ash Road) and continue along into the High Street. The ground is just past the Railway Bridge on the right; From the A31: Continue along the A31 to the junction with the A331, then as above; From the A325 (Farnborough Road): Follow signs to the A323 then turn left into Wellington Avenue. The ground is just off the 2nd roundabout on the left – the floodlights are clearly visible.

ALFRETON TOWN FC

Founded: 1959
Former Names: None
Nickname: 'Reds'
Ground: The Impact Arena, North Street, Alfreton, Derbyshire DE55 7FZ
Record Attendance: 5,023 vs Matlock Town (1960)
Pitch Size: 110 × 75 yards

Colours: Red shirts and shorts
Telephone Nº: (0115) 939-2090
Fax Number: (0115) 949-1846
Ground Capacity: 5,100
Seating Capacity: 1,600
Web site: www.alfretontownfc.com

GENERAL INFORMATION
Car Parking: At the ground
Coach Parking: Available close to the ground
Nearest Railway Station: Alfreton (½ mile)
Nearest Bus Station: Alfreton (5 minutes walk)
Club Shop: At the ground
Opening Times: Matchdays only
Telephone Nº: (01773) 830277

GROUND INFORMATION
Away Supporters' Entrances & Sections:
Segregation is usual so please check prior to the game

ADMISSION INFO (2014/2015 PRICES)
Adult Standing: £18.00
Adult Seating: £18.00
Senior Citizen Standing: £12.00
Senior Citizen Seating: £12.00
Under-16s Standing: £3.00 (with a paying adult)
Under-16s Seating: £3.00 (with a paying adult)

DISABLED INFORMATION
Wheelchairs: Accommodated in dedicated areas of the ground
Helpers: Admitted
Prices: Please phone the club for information
Disabled Toilets: Available
Contact: (01773) 830277 (Bookings are not necessary)

Travelling Supporters' Information:
Routes: Exit the M1 at Junction 28 and take the A38 signposted for Derby. After 2 miles take the sliproad onto the B600 then go right at the main road towards the town centre. After ½ mile turn left down North Street and the ground is on the right after 200 yards.

ALTRINCHAM FC

Founded: 1891
Former Names: Broadheath FC
Nickname: 'The Robins'
Ground: Moss Lane, Altrincham   WA15 8AP
Record Attendance: 10,275 (February 1925)
Pitch Size: 110 × 72 yards
Web site: www.altrinchamfc.com

Colours: Red and White striped shirts, Black shorts
Telephone Nº: (0161) 928-1045
Daytime Phone Nº: (0161) 928-1045
Fax Number: (0161) 926-9934
Ground Capacity: 6,085
Seating Capacity: 1,154
E-mail: office@altrinchamfootballclub.co.uk

GENERAL INFORMATION
Car Parking: Limited street parking
Coach Parking: By Police Direction
Nearest Railway Station: Altrincham (15 minutes walk)
Nearest Bus Station: Altrincham
Club Shop: Inside the ground
Opening Times: Matchdays only. Opens one hour prior to the start of the game.
Telephone Nº: (0161) 928-1045

GROUND INFORMATION
Away Supporters' Entrances & Sections:
Hale End turnstiles and accommodation

ADMISSION INFO (2014/2015 PRICES)
Adult Standing: £14.00
Adult Seating: £15.00
Concessionary Standing: £9.00
Concessionary Seating: £10.00
Ages 12-16 years Standing/Seating: £5.00
Under-12s Standing/Seating: £2.00

DISABLED INFORMATION
Wheelchairs: 3 spaces are available each for home and away fans adjacent to the Away dugout
Helpers: Admitted
Prices: Free for the disabled. £13.00 for helpers
Disabled Toilets: Yes
Contact: (0161) 928-1045   (Bookings are necessary)

Travelling Supporters' Information:
Routes: Exit the M56 at either Junction 6 or 7 and follow the signs for Altrincham FC.

BARNET FC

No photograph of the new ground
was available at the time of going to print.

Founded: 1888
Former Names: Barnet Alston FC
Nickname: 'The Bees'
Ground: The Hive, Camrose Avenue, Edgware, HA8 6AG
Record Attendance: –
Pitch Size: 112 × 73 yards

Colours: Shirts and shorts are Black with Amber Trim
Telephone No: (020) 8381-3800
Ticket Office: (020) 8381-3800
Fax Number: –
Ground Capacity: 5,176
Seating Capacity: 3,434
Web site: www.barnetfc.com
E-mail: info@barnetfc.com

GENERAL INFORMATION
Car Parking: 350 spaces available at the ground
Coach Parking: Available at the ground
Nearest Railway Station: Harrow & Wealdstone (2½ miles)
Nearest Tube Station: Canons Park (15 minutes walk)
Club Shop: At the ground
Opening Times: Monday to Friday 10.00am to 5.00pm and Saturday Matchdays from 11.00am to 5.00pm
Telephone No: (020) 8381-3800

GROUND INFORMATION
Away Supporters' Entrances & Sections:
North Terrace and North West corner

ADMISSION INFO (2014/2015 PRICES)
Adult Standing: £17.00
Adult Seating: £20.00 – £25.00
Concessionary Seating: £13.00 – £15.00
Junior Bees (Under-14s): £5.00 (Members only)
Happy 9s Club (Ages 9 and under): £2.00 (Members only)
Away Supporters: £17.00 Standing; £20.00 Seating
Programme Price: £3.00

DISABLED INFORMATION
Wheelchairs: 43 covered spaces in total for Home and Away fans in the East and West Stands
Helpers: One helper admitted per wheelchair
Prices: £20.00 for each fan with a wheelchair
Disabled Toilets: Available
Contact: (020) 8381-3800 (Bookings are not necessary)

Travelling Supporters' Information:
Routes: Exit the M1 at Junction 4 and take the Edgware Way/Watford Bypass (A41). Take the 3rd exit at the roundabout onto the A410 then the first exit at the next roundabout along the A5 (Stonegrove), continuing for approximately 1½ miles. Turn right into Camrose Avenue and The Hive is approximately two-thirds of a mile along this road.

BRAINTREE TOWN FC

Founded: 1898
Former Names: Manor Works FC, Crittall Athletic FC, Braintree & Crittall Athletic FC and Braintree FC
Nickname: 'The Iron'
Ground: Amlin Stadium, Clockhouse Way, Braintree, Essex CM7 3RD
Record Attendance: 4,000 (May 1952)
Pitch Size: 111 × 78 yards
Ground Capacity: 4,222
Seating Capacity: 556

Colours: Orange shirts and socks with Blue shorts
Telephone Nº: (01376) 345617
Fax Number: (01376) 330976
Correspondence Address: Tom Woodley, 19A Bailey Bridge Road, Braintree CM7 5TT
Contact Telephone Nº: (01376) 326234
Web site: www.braintreetownfc.org.uk
E-mail: braintreetfc@aol.com

GENERAL INFORMATION
Car Parking: At the ground
Coach Parking: At the ground
Nearest Railway Station: Braintree (1 mile)
Nearest Bus Station: Braintree
Club Shop: At the ground
Opening Times: Matchdays only
Telephone Nº: (01376) 345617

GROUND INFORMATION
Away Supporters' Entrances & Sections: Gates 7-8

ADMISSION INFO (2014/2015 PRICES)
Adult Standing: £15.00 – £17.00
Adult Seating: £16.00 – £18.00
Senior Citizen Standing: £11.00
Under-16s Standing: £6.00
Under-11s Standing: £4.00
Note: Prices vary depending on the category of the game

DISABLED INFORMATION
Wheelchairs: Accommodated – 6 spaces available in the Main Stand
Helpers: Admitted
Prices: Normal prices apply
Disabled Toilets: Available
Contact: (01376) 345617

Travelling Supporters' Information:
Routes: Exit the A120 Braintree Bypass at the McDonald's roundabout and follow Cressing Road northwards. The floodlights at the ground are visible on the left ½ mile into town. Turn left into Clockhouse Way then left again for the ground.

BRISTOL ROVERS FC

Founded: 1883 (**Entered League**: 1920)
Former Names: Black Arabs FC (1883-84);
Eastville Rovers FC (1884-96);
Bristol Eastville Rovers FC (1896-97)
Nickname: 'Pirates' 'Rovers' 'Gas'
Ground: Memorial Stadium, Filton Avenue, Horfield,
Bristol   BS7 0BF
Pitch Size: 110 × 71 yards

Ground Capacity: 11,917
Seating Capacity: 3,307
Record Attendance: 12,011 (9th March 2008)
Colours: Blue & White quartered shirts, White shorts
Telephone Nº: (0117) 909-6648
Fax Number: (0117) 907-4312
Web Site: www.bristolrovers.co.uk

GENERAL INFORMATION

Car Parking: Very limited number of spaces at the ground and street parking
Coach Parking: At the ground
Nearest Railway Station: Temple Meads (2 miles)
Nearest Bus Station: Bristol City Centre
Club Shop: 199 Two Mile Hill Road, Kingswood and also at Pirate Leisure, Memorial Stadium, Filton Avenue
Opening Times: Supporters' Club: Weekdays 9.00am to 5.00pm and Saturdays 9.00am to 1.00pm; Pirate Leisure: Weekdays 9.00am to 5.00pm, Saturdays 9.00am to 1.00pm (Home matchdays 9.00am – 3.00pm then 4.45pm – 5.15pm)
Telephone Nº: (0117) 961-1772 + (0117) 909-6648

GROUND INFORMATION

Away Supporters' Entrances & Sections:
Entrance to Uplands Terrace & South Stand via Filton Avenue

ADMISSION INFO (2014/2015 PRICES)

Adult Standing: £18.00 – £20.00
Adult Seating: £20.50 – £26.00
Concessionary Standing: £7.00 – £11.00
Concessionary Seating: £11.50 – £20.50
Note: A discount of £2.00 per ticket is available if purchased prior to the matchday.
Programme Price: £3.00

DISABLED INFORMATION

Wheelchairs: Unspecified number accommodated in front of the Uplands Stand and DAS Stand
Helpers: One helper admitted per disabled person
Prices: £11.00 for wheelchair and ambulant disabled. Helpers are admitted free of charge
Disabled Toilets: In the Uplands Stand and DAS Stand
Contact: (0117) 909-6648 Option 1 (Bookings are necessary)

Travelling Supporters' Information: Routes: From All Parts: Exit the M32 at Junction 2 then take the exit at the roundabout (signposted Horfield) into Muller Road. Continue for approximately 1½ miles passing straight across 3 sets of traffic lights. At the 6th set of traffic lights turn left into Filton Avenue and the ground is immediately on the left.

CHESTER FC

Founded: 1885
Former Names: Chester FC and Chester City FC
Nickname: 'City'
Ground: Exacta Centurion Community Stadium, Bumpers Lane, Chester   CH1 4LT
Pitch Size: 116 × 75 yards
Record Attendance: 5,987 (17th April 2004)

Colours: Blue and White striped shirts, Black shorts
Ground Telephone Nº: (01244) 371376
Ticket Office: (01244) 371376
Fax Number: (01244) 390265
Ground Capacity: 5,556
Seating Capacity: 4,170
Web site: www.chesterfc.com

GENERAL INFORMATION

Car Parking: Ample spaces available at the ground (£1.00)
Coach Parking: Available at the ground
Nearest Railway Station: Chester (2 miles)
Nearest Bus Station: Chester (1½ miles)
Club Shop: At the ground
Opening Times: Weekdays & matchdays 10.00am–4.00pm
Telephone Nº: (01244) 371376

GROUND INFORMATION

Away Supporters' Entrances & Sections:
South Stand for covered seating and also part of the West Stand

ADMISSION INFO (2014/2015 PRICES)

Adult Standing: £15.00
Adult Seating: £18.00
Senior Citizen Standing: £10.00
Senior Citizen Seating: £12.00
Under-21s Seating/Standing: £10.00
Under-16s Seating/Standing: £3.00 (Under-5s free)

DISABLED INFORMATION

Wheelchairs: 32 spaces for wheelchairs (with 40 helpers) in the West Stand and East Stand
Helpers: One helper admitted per disabled person
Prices: Concessionary prices for the disabled. Free for helpers
Disabled Toilets: Available in West and East Stands
Contact: (01244) 371376 (Bookings are necessary)

Travelling Supporters' Information:
Routes: From the North: Take the M56, A41 or A56 into the Town Centre and then follow Queensferry (A548) signs into Sealand Road. Turn left at the traffic lights by 'Tesco' into Bumpers Lane – the ground is ½ mile at the end of the road; From the East: Take the A54 or A51 into the Town Centre (then as North); From the South: Take the A41 or A483 into Town Centre (then as North); From the West: Take the A55, A494 or A548 and follow Queensferry signs towards Birkenhead (A494) and after 1¼ miles bear left onto the A548 (then as North); From the M6/M56 (Avoiding Town Centre): Take the M56 to Junction 16 (signposted Queensferry), turn left at the roundabout onto A5117, signposted Wales. At the next roundabout turn left onto the A5480 (signposted Chester) and after approximately 3 miles take the 3rd exit from the roundabout (signposted Sealand Road Industrial Parks). Go straight across 2 sets of traffic lights into Bumpers Lane. The ground is ½ mile on the right.

DARTFORD FC

Founded: 1888
Former Names: None
Nickname: 'The Darts'
Ground: Princes Park Stadium, Grassbanks, Darenth Road, Dartford DA1 1RT
Record Attendance: 4,097 (11th November 2006)
Pitch Size: 110 × 71 yards

Colours: White Shirts with Black Shorts
Telephone Nº: (01322) 299990
Fax Number: (01322) 299996
Ground Capacity: 4,097
Seating Capacity: 640
Web Site: www.dartfordfc.co.uk
E-mail: info@dartfordfc.co.uk

GENERAL INFORMATION

Car Parking: At the ground
Coach Parking: At the ground
Nearest Railway Station: Dartford (½ mile)
Nearest Bus Station: Dartford (½ mile) & Bluewater (2 miles)
Club Shop: At the ground
Opening Times: Matchdays only – 1.00pm to 6.00pm.
Telephone Nº: (01322) 299990

ADMISSION INFO (2014/2015 PRICES)

Adult Standing: £16.00
Adult Seating: £16.00
Senior Citizen/Concessionary Standing: £8.00
Senior Citizen/Concessionary Seating: £8.00
Under-12s Standing/Seating: £3.00
Under-5s Standing/Seating: Free of charge

DISABLED INFORMATION

Wheelchairs: Accommodated
Helpers: Admitted
Prices: Concessionary prices for the disabled and helpers
Disabled Toilets: Available
Contact: (01322) 299991 (Bookings are not necessary)

Travelling Supporters' Information:
Routes: From M25 Clockwise: Exit the M25 at Junction 1B. At the roundabout, take the 3rd exit onto Princes Road (A225) then the second exit at the next roundabout.* Continue downhill to the traffic lights (with the ground on the left), turn left into Darenth Road then take the 2nd left for the Car Park; From M25 Anti-clockwise: Exit the M25 at Junction 2 and follow the A225 to the roundabout. Take the first exit at this roundabout then the 2nd exit at the next roundabout. Then as from * above.

DOVER ATHLETIC FC

Founded: 1983
Former Names: None
Nickname: 'The Whites'
Ground: Crabble Athletic Ground, Lewisham Road, River, Dover CT17 0JB
Record Attendance: 4,186 (2002)
Pitch Size: 111 × 73 yards

Colours: White shirts with Black shorts
Telephone Nº: (01304) 822373
Fax Number: (01304) 821383
Ground Capacity: 6,500
Seating Capacity: 1,000
Web site: www.doverathletic.com
E-mail: enquiries@doverathletic.com

GENERAL INFORMATION

Car Parking: Street parking
Coach Parking: Street parking
Nearest Railway Station: Kearsney (1 mile)
Nearest Bus Station: Pencester Road, Dover (1½ miles)
Club Shop: At the ground
Opening Times: Saturdays 9.00am to 12.00pm
Telephone Nº: (01304) 822373

GROUND INFORMATION

Away Supporters' Entrances & Sections:
Segregation only used when required

ADMISSION INFO (2014/2015 PRICES)

Adult Standing: £15.00
Adult Seating: £16.50
Senior Citizen Standing: £12.00
Senior Citizen Seating: £14.00
Under-18s Standing: £6.00
Under-18s Seating: £7.50
Under-11s Standing/Seating: Free of charge

DISABLED INFORMATION

Wheelchairs: Approximately 20 spaces are available in front of the Family Stand
Helpers: Please phone the club for information
Prices: Please phone the club for information
Disabled Toilets: None
Contact: –   (Bookings are not necessary)

Travelling Supporters' Information:
Routes: Take the A2 to the Whitfield roundabout and take the 4th exit. Travel down the hill to the mini-roundabout then turn left and follow the road for 1 mile to the traffic lights on the hill. Turn sharp right and pass under the railway bridge – the ground is on the left after 300 yards.

EASTLEIGH FC

Founded: 1946
Former Names: Swaythling Athletic FC and Swaythling FC
Nickname: 'The Spitfires'
Ground: Silverlake Stadium, Ten Acres, Stoneham Lane, Eastleigh SO50 9HT
Record Attendance: 3,104 (2006)
Pitch Size: 112 × 74 yards

Colours: Blue shirts with White shorts
Telephone Nº: (023) 8061-3361
Fax Number: (023) 8061-2379
Ground Capacity: 6,000
Seating Capacity: 2,812 (by October 2014)
Web site: www.eastleighfc.com
e-mail: admin@eastleighfc.com

GENERAL INFORMATION

Car Parking: Spaces for 450 cars available (hard standing)
Coach Parking: At the ground
Nearest Railway Station: Southampton Parkway (¾ mile)
Nearest Bus Station: Eastleigh (2 miles)
Club Shop: At the ground
Opening Times: Matchdays and during functions only

GROUND INFORMATION

Away Supporters' Entrances & Sections:
Segregation in force for some games only. Please contact the club for further details

ADMISSION INFO (2014/2015 PRICES)

Adult Standing: £12.00
Adult Seating: £15.00
Concessionary Standing: £7.50
Concessionary Seating: £10.00
Under-16s Standing/Seating: £4.00
Under-7s Standing/Seating: Free of charge

DISABLED INFORMATION

Wheelchairs: Accommodated
Helpers: Admitted
Prices: Concessionary prices apply
Disabled Toilets: Available
Contact: (023) 8061-3361 (Bookings are not necessary)

Travelling Supporters' Information:
Routes: Exit the M27 at Junction 5 (signposted for Southampton Airport) and take the A335 (Stoneham Way) towards Southampton. After ½ mile, turn right at the traffic lights into Bassett Green Road. Turn right at the next set of traffic lights into Stoneham Lane and the ground is on the right after ¾ mile.

FC HALIFAX TOWN

Founded: 1911 (Re-formed 2008)
Former Names: Halifax Town FC
Nickname: 'The Shaymen'
Ground: The Shay Stadium, Shay Syke, Halifax, HX1 2YT
Ground Capacity: 10,568
Seating Capacity: 5,285

Record Attendance: 4,023 (1st January 2011)
Pitch Size: 112 × 73 yards
Colours: Blue shirts and shorts
Telephone Nº: (01422) 341222
Fax Number: (01422) 349487
Web Site: www.halifaxafc.co.uk
E-mail: secretary@halifaxafc.co.uk

GENERAL INFORMATION
Car Parking: Adjacent to the East Stand and also Shaw Hill Car Park (Nearby)
Coach Parking: By arrangement with the Club Secretary
Nearest Railway Station: Halifax (10 minutes walk)
Nearest Bus Station: Halifax (15 minutes walk)
Club Shop: At the ground in the East Stand
Opening Times: Please phone for details
Telephone Nº: (01422) 341222 (to change during the 2011/12 season)

GROUND INFORMATION
Away Supporters' Entrances & Sections:
Skircoat Stand (Seating only)

ADMISSION INFO (2014/2015 PRICES)
Adult Standing/Seating: £17.00
Under-16s Standing/Seating: £6.00
Senior Citizen Standing/Seating: £13.00
Under-12s Standing/Seating: £6.00
Under-7s Standing/Seating: £3.00

DISABLED INFORMATION
Wheelchairs: 33 spaces available in total in disabled sections in the East Stand and South Stand
Helpers: One admitted free with each paying disabled fan
Prices: Free of charge for the disabled and helpers
Disabled Toilets: Available in the East and South Stands
Contact: (01422) 434212 (Bookings are not necessary)

Travelling Supporters' Information:
Routes: From the North: Take the A629 to Halifax Town Centre. Take the 2nd exit at the roundabout into Broad Street and follow signs for Huddersfield (A629) into Skircoat Road; From the South, East and West: Exit the M62 at Junction 24 and follow Halifax (A629) signs for the Town Centre into Skircoat Road then Shaw Hill for ground.

FOREST GREEN ROVERS FC

Founded: 1889
Former Names: Stroud FC
Nickname: 'The Rovers'
Ground: The New Lawn, Smiths Way,
Forest Green, Nailsworth, Gloucestershire, GL6 0FG
Record Attendance: 4,836 (3rd January 2009)
Pitch Size: 110 × 70 yards

Colours: Black and White striped shirts, Black shorts
Telephone Nº: (01453) 834860
Fax Number: (01453) 835291
Ground Capacity: 5,147
Seating Capacity: 2,500
Web site: www.forestgreenroversfc.com
E-mail: reception@forestgreenroversfc.com

GENERAL INFORMATION

Car Parking: At the ground
Coach Parking: At the ground
Nearest Railway Station: Stroud (4 miles)
Nearest Bus Station: Nailsworth
Club Shop: At the ground
Opening Times: Matchdays only
Telephone Nº: (01453) 834860

GROUND INFORMATION

Away Supporters' Entrances & Sections:
EESI Stand

ADMISSION INFO (2014/2015 PRICES)

Adult Standing: £15.00   **Adult Seating**: £17.00–£19.00
Senior Citizen Standing: £11.00
Senior Citizen Seating: £13.00 – £15.00
Child Standing: £4.00   **Child Seating**: £5.00
Young Adult Standing: £7.00
Young Adult Seating: £9.00 – £11.00

DISABLED INFORMATION

Wheelchairs: Accommodated in the Main Stand
Helpers: Admitted
Prices: Normal prices for the disabled. Free for helpers
Disabled Toilets: Yes
Contact: (01453) 834860   (Enquiries necessary at least 72 hours in advance)

Travelling Supporters' Information:
Routes: The ground is located 4 miles south of Stroud on the A46 to Bath. Upon entering Nailsworth, turn into Spring Hill at the mini-roundabout and the ground is approximately ½ mile up the hill on the left.

GATESHEAD FC

Founded: 1930   (Reformed in 1977)
Former Names: Gateshead United FC
Nickname: 'Tynesiders'
Ground: International Stadium, Neilson Road, Gateshead   NE10 0EF
Record Attendance: 11,750 (1995)
Pitch Size: 110 × 70 yards

Colours: White shirts with Black shorts
Telephone Nº: (0191) 478-3883
Fax Number: (0191) 440-0404
Ground Capacity: 11,750
Seating Capacity: 11,750
Web site: www.gateshead-fc.com
E-mail: info@gateshead-fc.com

GENERAL INFORMATION
Car Parking: At the stadium
Coach Parking: At the stadium
Nearest Railway Station: Gateshead Stadium Metro (½ mile); Newcastle (British Rail) 1½ miles
Nearest Bus Station: Heworth Interchange (½ mile)
Club Shop: At the stadium
Opening Times: Matchdays only
Telephone Nº: (0191) 478-3883

GROUND INFORMATION
Away Supporters' Entrances & Sections:
Tyne & Wear County Stand North End or the East Stand

ADMISSION INFO (2014/2015 PRICES)
Adult Seating: £15.00
Senior Citizen/Concessionary Seating: £10.00
Under-16s Seating: £3.00
Under-18s/Student Seating: £8.00
Note: Tickets are cheaper when purchased in advance.

DISABLED INFORMATION
Wheelchairs: 5 spaces available each for home and away fans by the trackside – Level access with automatic doors
Helpers: Admitted
Prices: Normal prices for the disabled. Helpers are admitted free of charge.
Disabled Toilets: Available in the Reception Area and on the 1st floor concourse – accessible by lift.
Contact: (0191) 478-3883   (Bookings are necessary)

Travelling Supporters' Information:
Routes: From the South: Take the A1(M) to Washington Services and fork right onto the A194(M) signposted Tyne Tunnel. At the next roundabout, turn left onto the A184 signposted for Gateshead. The Stadium is on the right after 3 miles.

GRIMSBY TOWN FC

Founded: 1878
Former Names: Grimsby Pelham FC (1879)
Nickname: 'Mariners'
Ground: Blundell Park, Cleethorpes   DN35 7PY
Ground Capacity: 8,974 (All seats)
Record Attendance: 31,651 (20th February 1937)
Pitch Size: 111 × 74 yards

Colours: Black and White striped shirts, Black shorts
Telephone Nº: (01472) 605050
Ticket Office: (01472) 605050
Fax Number: (01472) 693665
Web Site: www.grimsby-townfc.co.uk
E-mail: info@gtfc.co.uk

GENERAL INFORMATION

Car Parking: Street parking
Coach Parking: Harrington Street – near the ground
Nearest Railway Station: Cleethorpes (1½ miles)
Nearest Bus Station: Brighowgate, Grimsby (4 miles)
Club Shop: At the ground
Opening Times: Monday – Friday 9.00am to 5.00pm;
Matchday Saturdays 9.00am to kick-off
Telephone Nº: (01472) 605050

GROUND INFORMATION

Away Supporters' Entrances & Sections:
Harrington Street turnstiles 15-18 and Constitution Avenue
turnstiles 5-14

ADMISSION INFO (2014/2015 PRICES)

Adult Seating: £18.00 (Away fans £18.00)
Senior Citizen/Student Seating: £12.00
Young Adults Seating (Ages 15–18): £12.00
Child Seating: £4.00 – £6.00 (Under-15s)
Note: Tickets are cheaper if purchased before the matchday

DISABLED INFORMATION

Wheelchairs: 50 spaces in total for Home and Away fans in
the disabled section, in front of the Main Stand
Helpers: Helpers are admitted
Prices: £18.00 for the disabled. Free of charge for helpers
Disabled Toilets: Available in disabled section
Commentaries are available in disabled section
Contact: (01472) 605050   (Bookings are necessary)

Travelling Supporters' Information:
Routes: From All Parts except Lincolnshire and East Anglia: Take the M180 to the A180 and follow signs for Grimsby/
Cleethorpes. The A180 ends at a roundabout (the 3rd in short distance after crossing docks), take the 2nd exit from the roundabout
over the Railway flyover into Cleethorpes Road (A1098) and continue into Grimsby Road. After the second stretch of dual
carriageway, the ground is ½ mile on the left; From Lincolnshire: Take the A46 or A16 and follow Cleethorpes signs along
(A1098) Weelsby Road for 2 miles. Take the 1st exit at the roundabout at the end of Clee Road into Grimsby Road. The ground is
1¾ miles on the right.

KIDDERMINSTER HARRIERS FC

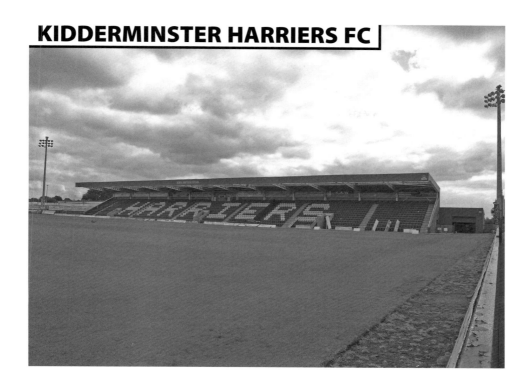

Founded: 1886
Nickname: 'Harriers'
Ground: Aggborough, Hoo Road, Kidderminster, Worcestershire   DY10 1NB
Ground Capacity: 6,444
Seating Capacity: 3,143
Record Attendance: 9,155 (1948)

Pitch Size: 110 × 72 yards
Colours: Red shirts and shorts
Telephone Nº: (01562) 823931
Fax Number: (01562) 827329
Web Site: www.harriers.co.uk
E-mail: info@harriers.co.uk

GENERAL INFORMATION
Car Parking: At the ground
Coach Parking: As directed
Nearest Railway Station: Kidderminster
Nearest Bus Station: Kidderminster Town Centre
Club Shop: At the ground
Opening Times: Weekdays and First Team Matchdays 9.00am to 5.00pm
Telephone Nº: (01562) 823931

GROUND INFORMATION
Away Supporters' Entrances & Sections:
John Smiths Stand Entrance D and South Terrace Entrance E

ADMISSION INFO (2014/2015 PRICES)
Adult Standing: £14.00
Adult Seating: £17.00
Senior Citizen Standing: £8.00
Senior Citizen Seating: £11.00
Under-16s Standing: £5.00
Under-16s Seating: £8.00
Note: Under-5s are admitted free with a paying adult

DISABLED INFORMATION
Wheelchairs: Home fans accommodated at the front of the Main Stand, Away fans in front of the John Smiths Stand
Helpers: Admitted
Prices: £10.00 for each disabled fan plus one helper
Disabled Toilets: Available by the disabled area
Contact: (01562) 823931   (Bookings are not necessary)

Travelling Supporters' Information:
Routes: Exit the M5 at Junction 3 and follow the A456 to Kidderminster. The ground is situated close by the Severn Valley Railway Station so follow the brown Steam Train signs and turn into Hoo Road about 200 yards downhill of the station. Follow the road along for ¼ mile and the ground is on the left.

LINCOLN CITY FC

Founded: 1884
Nickname: 'Red Imps'
Ground: Sincil Bank Stadium, Lincoln LN5 8LD
Ground Capacity: 10,120 (All seats)
Record Attendance: 23,196 (15th November 1967)
Pitch Size: 110 × 72 yards

Colours: Red and White striped shirts, Black shorts
Telephone Nº: (01522) 880011
Ticket Office: (01522) 880011
Fax Number: (01522) 880020
Web Site: www.redimps.co.uk

GENERAL INFORMATION

Car Parking: Stacey West Car Park (limited parking for £5.00 per car).
Coach Parking: Please contact the club for details.
Nearest Railway Station: Lincoln Central
Club Shop: At the ground
Opening Times: Weekdays 10.00am to 2.00pm and Saturday Matchdays 10.00am until kick-off and 30 minutes after the final whistle
Telephone Nº: (01522) 880011

GROUND INFORMATION

Away Supporters' Entrances & Sections:
Lincolnshire Co-operative Stand (seated) – Turnstiles 24 & 25

ADMISSION INFO (2014/2015 PRICES)

Adult Seating: £18.00
Junior Seating: £7.00
Concessionary Seating: £13.00
Note: Prices vary depending on the category of the game and area of the ground. Discounts are available for families and for advance ticket purchases

DISABLED INFORMATION

Wheelchairs: Limited number of spaces available in the disabled section, adjacent to turnstile 23
Helpers: One helper admitted per disabled person
Prices: Applications for disabled passes must be made to the club. Wheelchair-bound disabled are charged concessionary prices. Helpers are admitted free if the disabled fan has a medium/high level disability allowance
Disabled Toilets: Adjacent to disabled area
Contact: (01522) 880011 (Bookings are necessary)

Travelling Supporters' Information:
Routes: From the East: Take the A46 or A158 into the City Centre following Newark (A46) signs into the High Street and take next left (Scorer Street and Cross Street) for the ground; From the North and West: Take the A15 or A57 into the City Centre, then as from the East; From the South: Take the A1 then A46 for the City Centre, then into the High Street, parking on the South Common or in the Stadium via South Park Avenue, turn down by the Fire Station.

MACCLESFIELD TOWN FC

Founded: 1874
Former Names: Macclesfield FC
Nickname: 'The Silkmen'
Ground: Moss Rose Ground, London Road, Macclesfield, Cheshire SK11 7SP
Ground Capacity: 5,977
Seating Capacity: 2,599
Record Attendance: 10,041 (1948)

Pitch Size: 110 × 66 yards
Colours: Blue shirts, White shorts and Blue socks
Telephone Nº: (01625) 264686
Ticket Office: (01625) 264686
Fax Number: (01625) 264692
Web Site: www.mtfc.co.uk
E-mail: office@mtfc.co.uk

GENERAL INFORMATION

Car Parking: Ample parking available near the ground
Coach Parking: Near the ground
Nearest Railway Station: Macclesfield (1 mile)
Nearest Bus Station: Macclesfield
Club Shop: At the ground
Opening Times: Weekdays and matchdays 9.00am to 5.00pm
Telephone Nº: (01625) 264686

GROUND INFORMATION

Away Supporters' Entrances & Sections:
John Askey Terrace and the left side of the Moss Lane Stand

ADMISSION INFO (2014/2015 PRICES)

Adult Standing: £14.00
Adult Seating: £18.00
Concessions Standing: £10.00
Concessions Seating: £14.00
Under-12s Standing: £3.00
Under-12s Seating: £3.00
Ages 12-15 Standing: £5.00
Ages 12-15 Seating: £5.00

DISABLED INFORMATION

Wheelchairs: 45 spaces in front of the Estate Road Stand
Helpers: One helper admitted per disabled fan
Prices: Normal prices apply for the disabled. Helpers are admitted free of charge
Disabled Toilets: 3 available
Contact: (01625) 264686 (Bookings are necessary)

Travelling Supporters' Information:
Routes: From the North: Exit the M6 at Junction 19 to Knutsford, follow the A537 to Macclesfield. Follow signs for the Town Centre, then for the A523 to Leek. The ground is 1 mile out of the Town Centre on the right; From the South: Exit M6 at Junction 17 for Sandbach and follow the A534 to Congleton. Then take the A536 to Macclesfield. After passing The Rising Sun on the left, ¼ mile further on turn right after the Texaco Garage (Moss Lane). Following this lane will bring you back to the ground.

NUNEATON TOWN FC

Founded: 1937 (Reformed 2008)
Former Names: Nuneaton Borough FC
Nickname: 'Boro'
Ground: Sperrin Brewery Stadium, Liberty Way, Attleborough Fields Industrial Estate, Nuneaton, CV11 6RR
Record Attendance: 3,111 (2nd May 2009)
Pitch Size: 109 × 74 yards

Colours: Blue shirts and white shorts
Telephone Nº: (024) 7638-5738
Fax Number: (024) 7637-2995
Ground Capacity: 4,500
Seating Capacity: 500
Web site: www.nuneatontownfc.com
E-mail: admin@nuneatontownfc.com

GENERAL INFORMATION

Car Parking: On-site car park plus various other parking spaces available on the nearby Industrial Estate
Coach Parking: At the ground
Nearest Railway Station: Nuneaton (2 miles)
Nearest Bus Station: Nuneaton (2 miles)
Club Shop: Yes – The Boro Shop
Opening Times: By appointment and also on matchdays
Telephone Nº: (024) 7638-5738

GROUND INFORMATION

Away Supporters' Entrances & Sections:
No usual segregation

ADMISSION INFO (2014/2015 PRICES)

Adult Standing: £14.00
Adult Seating: £16.00
Concessionary Standing: £14.00
Concessionary Seating: £16.00
Under-16s Standing: £3.00
Under-16s Seating: £5.00

DISABLED INFORMATION

Wheelchairs: Accommodated, but only 5 spaces are available
Helpers: Admitted
Prices: Normal prices apply for the disabled and helpers
Disabled Toilets: Available
Contact: (024) 7638-5738   (Bookings are necessary)

Travelling Supporters' Information:
Routes: From the South, West and North-West: Exit the M6 at Junction 3 and follow the A444 into Nuneaton. At the Coton Arches roundabout turn right into Avenue Road which is the A4254 signposted for Hinckley. Continue along the A4254 following the road into Garrett Street then Eastboro Way then turn left into Townsend Drive. Follow the road round before turning left into Liberty Way for the ground; From the North: Exit the M1 at Junction 21 and follow the M69. Exit the M69 at Junction 1 and take the 4th exit at the roundabout onto the A5 (Tamworth, Nuneaton). At Longshoot Junction, turn left onto the A47, continue to the roundabout and take the 1st exit onto A4254 Eastborough Way. Turn right at the next roundabout into Townsend Drive then immediately right again for Liberty Way.

SOUTHPORT FC

Founded: 1881
Former Names: Southport Vulcan FC, Southport Central FC
Nickname: 'The Sandgrounders'
Ground: Merseyrail Community Stadium, Haig Avenue, Southport, Merseyside   PR8 6JZ
Record Attendance: 20,010 (1932)
Pitch Size: 110 × 77 yards

Colours: Yellow shirts and shorts
Telephone N°: (01704) 533422
Fax Number: (01704) 533455
Ground Capacity: 6,008
Seating Capacity: 1,660
Web site: www.southportfc.net

GENERAL INFORMATION
Car Parking: Street parking
Coach Parking: Adjacent to the ground
Nearest Railway Station: Meols Cop (½ mile)
Nearest Bus Station: Southport Town Centre
Club Shop: At the ground
Opening Times: Matchdays from 1.30pm (from 6.30pm on evening matchdays)
Telephone N°: (01704) 533422

GROUND INFORMATION
Away Supporters' Entrances & Sections:
Blowick End entrances

ADMISSION INFO (2014/2015 PRICES)
Adult Standing: £13.50
Adult Seating: £15.00
Concessionary Standing: £10.00
Concessionary Seating: £11.00
Under-19s Standing/Seating: £5.00
Note: Children aged 11 and under are admitted free of charge when accompanied by a paying adult.

DISABLED INFORMATION
Wheelchairs: Accommodated in front of the Grandstand
Helpers: Admitted
Prices: Concessionary prices charged for the disabled. Helpers are admitted free of charge
Disabled Toilets: Available at the Blowick End of the Grandstand
Contact: (01704) 533422   (Bookings are not necessary)

Travelling Supporters' Information:
Routes: Exit the M58 at Junction 3 and take the A570 to Southport. At the major roundabout (McDonalds/Tesco) go straight on into Scarisbrick New Road, pass over the brook and turn right into Haig Avenue at the traffic lights. The ground is then on the right-hand side.

TORQUAY UNITED FC

Founded: 1899 (**First Entered League**: 1927)
Former Name: Torquay Town FC (1899-1910)
Nickname: 'Gulls'
Ground: Plainmoor Ground, Torquay TQ1 3PS
Ground Capacity: 6,200 **Seating Capacity**: 2,841
Record Attendance: 21,908 (29th January 1955)
Pitch Size: 112 × 72 yards

Colours: Shirts are Yellow with a White stripe, shorts and socks are White
Telephone Nº: (01803) 328666 (Option 0)
Ticket Office: (01803) 328666 (Option 0)
Fax Number: (01803) 323976
Web Site: www.torquayunited.com
E-mail: reception@torquayunited.com

GENERAL INFORMATION
Car Parking: Street parking
Coach Parking: Lymington Road Coach Station (½ mile)
Nearest Railway Station: Torquay (2 miles)
Nearest Bus Station: Lymington Road (½ mile)
Club Shop: At the ground
Opening Times: Matchdays and during Office Hours
Telephone Nº: (01803) 328666 Option 0

GROUND INFORMATION
Away Supporters' Entrances & Sections:
Babbacombe End turnstiles for Babbacombe End

ADMISSION INFO (2014/2015 PRICES)
Adult Standing: £17.00
Adult Seating: £19.00 – £21.00
Concessionary Standing: £13.00
Concessionary Seating: £15.00 – £17.00
Under-16s Standing/Seating: £6.00
Note: Family tickets are also available
Programme Price: £3.00

DISABLED INFORMATION
Wheelchairs: 9 spaces in front of Bristow Bench Stand for home supporters plus 9 spaces in the Away end.
Helpers: One helper admitted per wheelchair
Prices: Normal prices for the disabled. Free for helpers
Disabled Toilets: Available in the Ellacombe End and the Away End
Audio facilities are available for the blind from reception
Contact: (01803) 328666 Option 0
(Bookings are necessary for the blind)

Travelling Supporters' Information:
Routes: From the North and East: Take the M5 to the A38 then A380 to Torquay. On entering Torquay, turn left at the 1st set of traffic lights after Riviera Way Retail Park into Hele Road. Following signs for the ground, continue straight on over two mini-roundabouts, go up West Hill Road to the traffic lights, then straight ahead into Warbro Road. The ground is situated on the right after 200 yards.

WELLING UNITED FC

Founded: 1963
Former Names: None
Nickname: 'The Wings'
Ground: Park View Road Ground, Welling, Kent, DA16 1SY
Record Attendance: 4,020 (1989/90)
Pitch Size: 112 × 72 yards

Colours: Shirts are Red with White facings, Red shorts
Telephone Nº: (0208) 301-1196
Daytime Phone Nº: (0208) 301-1196
Fax Number: (0208) 301-5676
Ground Capacity: 4,000
Seating Capacity: 500
Web site: www.wellingunited.com

GENERAL INFORMATION
Car Parking: Street parking only
Coach Parking: Outside of the ground
Nearest Railway Station: Welling (¾ mile)
Nearest Bus Station: Bexleyheath
Club Shop: At the ground
Opening Times: Matchdays only
Telephone Nº: (0208) 301-1196

GROUND INFORMATION
Away Supporters' Entrances & Sections:
Accommodation in the Danson Park End

ADMISSION INFO (2014/2015 PRICES)
Adult Standing: £15.00
Adult Seating: £16.00
Concessionary Standing: £9.00 – £10.00
Concessionary Seating: £10.00 – £11.00
Under-12s Standing: Free with a paying adult
Under-12s Seating: £1.00 with a paying adult

DISABLED INFORMATION
Wheelchairs: Accommodated at the side of the Main Stand
Helpers: Admitted
Prices: £7.50 for the disabled. Helpers pay normal prices
Disabled Toilets: Yes
Contact: (0208) 301-1196 (Bookings are not necessary)

Travelling Supporters' Information:
Routes: Take the A2 (Rochester Way) from London, then the A221 Northwards (Danson Road) to Bexleyheath. At the end turn left towards Welling along Park View Road and the ground is on the left.

WOKING FC

Founded: 1889
Former Names: None
Nickname: 'Cardinals'
Ground: Kingfield Stadium, Kingfield, Woking, Surrey GU22 9AA
Record Attendance: 6,000 (1997)
Pitch Size: 109 × 76 yards

Colours: Shirts are Red & White halves, Black shorts
Telephone Nº: (01483) 772470
Daytime Phone Nº: (01483) 772470
Fax Number: (01483) 888423
Ground Capacity: 6,161
Seating Capacity: 2,511
Web site: www.wokingfc.co.uk
E-mail: admin@wokingfc.co.uk

GENERAL INFORMATION
Car Parking: Limited parking at the ground
Coach Parking: At or opposite the ground
Nearest Railway Station: Woking (1 mile)
Nearest Bus Station: Woking
Club Shop: At the ground
Opening Times: Weekdays and Matchdays
Telephone Nº: (01483) 772470

GROUND INFORMATION
Away Supporters' Entrances & Sections:
Kingfield Road entrance for the Tennis Club terrace

ADMISSION INFO (2014/2015 PRICES)
Adult Standing: £15.00
Adult Seating: £15.00
Under-16s/Student Standing: £3.00
Under-16s/Student Seating: £3.00
Senior Citizen Standing: £10.00
Senior Citizen Seating: £10.00

DISABLED INFORMATION
Wheelchairs: 8 spaces in the Leslie Gosden Stand and 8 spaces in front of the Family Stand
Helpers: Admitted
Prices: One wheelchair and helper for £10.00
Disabled Toilets: Yes – in the Leslie Gosden Stand and Family Stand area
Contact: (01483) 772470 (Bookings are necessary)

Travelling Supporters' Information:
Routes: Exit the M25 at Junction 10 and follow the A3 towards Guildford. Leave at the next junction onto the B2215 through Ripley and join the A247 to Woking. Alternatively, exit the M25 at Junction 11 and follow the A320 to Woking Town Centre. The ground is on the outskirts of Woking – follow signs on the A320 and A247.

WREXHAM FC

Founded: 1864
Nickname: 'Red Dragons'
Ground: Racecourse Ground, Mold Road, Wrexham, North Wales   LL11 2AH
Ground Capacity: 10,500 (all seats)
Record Attendance: 34,445 (26th January 1957)
Pitch Size: 111 × 71 yards

Colours: Red shirts with White shorts
Telephone Nº: (01978) 262129
Fax Number: (01978) 357821
Web Site: www.wrexhamafc.co.uk
E-mail: info@wrexhamfc.tv

GENERAL INFORMATION

Car Parking: Town car parks are nearby and also Glyndwr University (Mold End)
Coach Parking: By Police direction
Nearest Railway Station: Wrexham General (adjacent)
Nearest Bus Station: Wrexham (King Street)
Club Shop: At the ground in the Yale Stand
Opening Times: Monday to Saturday 9.00am to 5.00pm
Telephone Nº: (01978) 262129

GROUND INFORMATION

Away Supporters' Entrances & Sections:
Turnstiles 1-4 for the Yale Stand

ADMISSION INFO (2014/2015 PRICES)

Adult Seating: £15.00 – £19.00
Under-16s Seating: £6.00 – £7.00
Under-11s Seating: £1.00 (with a paying adult)
Concessionary Seating: £12.00 – £14.00
Over-80s Seating: £6.00 – £7.00
Note: Family tickets are also available

DISABLED INFORMATION

Wheelchairs: 35 spaces in the Mold Road Stand
Helpers: One helper admitted per wheelchair
Prices: Normal prices for the disabled. Free for helpers
Disabled Toilets: Available in the disabled section
Contact: (01978) 262129   (Bookings are preferred)

Travelling Supporters' Information:
Routes: From the North and West: Take the A483 and the Wrexham bypass to the junction with the A541. Branch left at the roundabout and follow Wrexham signs into Mold Road; From the East: Take the A525 or A534 into Wrexham then follow the A541 signs into Mold Road; From the South: Take the the M6, then the M54 and follow the A5 and A483 to the Wrexham bypass and the junction with the A541. Branch right at the roundabout and follow signs for the Town Centre.

THE FOOTBALL CONFERENCE NORTH

Address

4th Floor, 20 Waterloo Street,
Birmingham   B2 5TB

Phone (0121) 643-3143

Web site   www.footballconference.co.uk

Clubs for the 2014/2015 Season

AFC FYLDE

Founded: 1988
Former Names: Formed by the amalgamation of Wesham FC and Kirkham Town FC in 1988
Nickname: 'The Coasters'
Ground: Kellamergh Park, Bryning Lane, Warton, Preston   PR4 1TN
Record Attendance: 1,418 (13th October 2013)

Colours: White shirts and shorts
Telephone Nº: (01772) 682593
Fax Number: (01772) 685893
Ground Capacity: 3,000
Seating Capacity: 282
Pitch Size: 110 × 82 yards
Web Site: www.afcfylde.co.uk

GENERAL INFORMATION
Car Parking: At the ground
Coach Parking: At the ground
Nearest Railway Station: Moss Side (2¼ miles)
Club Shop: 6 Station Road, Kirkham   PR4 2AS
Opening Times: Matchdays only
Telephone Nº: (01772) 682593 (Phone orders accepted)

GROUND INFORMATION
Away Supporters' Entrances & Sections:
No usual segregation

ADMISSION INFO (2014/2015 PRICES)
Adult Standing: £10.00
Adult Seating: £10.00
Concessionary Standing: £7.00
Concessionary Seating: £7.00
Under-16s Standing: Free of charge
Under-16s Seating: Free of charge
Programme Price: £2.00

DISABLED INFORMATION
Wheelchairs: Accommodated
Helpers: Admitted
Prices: Normal prices apply for the disabled. Helpers pay concessionary prices
Disabled Toilets: None
Contact: (01772) 682593   (Bookings are not necessary)

Travelling Supporters' Information:
Routes: Exit the M55 at Junction 3 and take the A585 (signposted Fleetwood/Kirkham). At the roundabout outside of Kirkham, take the 2nd exit continuing on the A585, go straight on at the next roundabout, then at the roundabout junction with the A583, take the 2nd exit onto the B5259 Ribby Road. Follow this road into Wrea Green, then turn left by the Green itself into Bryning Lane. Continue for about 1 mile and the ground is situated on the left of the road.

BARROW FC

Founded: 1901
Former Names: None
Nickname: 'Bluebirds'
Ground: Furness Building Society Stadium, Barrow-in-Furness, Cumbria LA14 5UW
Record Attendance: 16,874 (1954)
Pitch Size: 110 × 75 yards

Colours: White shirts with Blue shorts
Telephone Nº: (01229) 823061
Fax Number: (01229) 823061
Ground Capacity: 4,057
Seating Capacity: 928
Web site: www.barrowafc.com
E-mail: office@barrowafc.com

GENERAL INFORMATION
Car Parking: Street Parking, Popular Side Car Park and Soccer Bar Car Park
Coach Parking: Adjacent to the ground
Nearest Railway Station: Barrow Central (½ mile)
Nearest Bus Station: ½ mile
Club Shop: At the ground
Opening Times: Monday to Friday 9.00am – 3.30pm and Saturdays 10.00am – 2.00pm
Telephone Nº: (01229) 823061

GROUND INFORMATION
Away Supporters' Entrances & Sections:
West Terrace (not covered)

ADMISSION INFO (2014/2015 PRICES)
Adult Standing: £13.00
Adult Seating: £14.00
Concessionary Standing: £10.00
Concessionary Seating: £11.00
Under-18s Standing/Seating: £5.00
Under-7s Standing/Seating: £1.00

DISABLED INFORMATION
Wheelchairs: 6 spaces available in the Disabled Area
Helpers: Admitted
Prices: Normal prices apply
Disabled Toilets: Available
Contact: (01229) 823061   (Bookings are not necessary)

Travelling Supporters' Information:
Routes: Exit the M6 at Junction 36 and take the A590 through Ulverston. Using the bypass, follow signs for Barrow. After approximately 5 miles, turn left into Wilkie Road and the ground is on the right.

BOSTON UNITED FC

Founded: 1933
Former Names: Boston Town FC & Boston Swifts FC
Nickname: 'The Pilgrims'
Ground: Jakeman's Stadium, York Street, Boston, PE21 6JN
Ground Capacity: 6,613 **Seating Capacity**: 2,000
Pitch Size: 112 × 72 yards

Record Attendance: 10,086 (1955)
Colours: Amber and Black shirts, Black shorts
Telephone Nº: (01205) 364406 (Office)
Matchday Info: (01205) 364406 or 07860 663299
Fax Number: (01205) 354063
Web Site: www.bufc.co.uk
E-mail: admin@bufc.co.uk

GENERAL INFORMATION
Car Parking: Permit holders only
Coach Parking: Available near to the ground
Nearest Railway Station: Boston (1 mile)
Nearest Bus Station: Boston Coach Station (¼ mile)
Club Shop: In the car park at the ground
Opening Times: Weekdays from 9.00am to 5.00pm and Saturday Matchdays from 11.00am to 5.00pm
Telephone Nº: (01205) 364406

GROUND INFORMATION
Away Supporters' Entrances & Sections:
York Street Entrances 3 & 4 (subject to a move to the Jakemans Stand if so advised by the police)

ADMISSION INFO (2014/2015 PRICES)
Adult Standing: £12.00
Adult Seating: £14.00
Child Standing: £4.00
Child Seating: £5.00
Senior Citizen Standing: £9.00
Senior Citizen Seating: £10.00

DISABLED INFORMATION
Wheelchairs: 7 spaces available for home fans, 4 spaces for away fans below the Main Stand at the Town End
Helpers: One helper admitted per disabled fan
Prices: £12.00 for the disabled. Free of charge for helpers
Disabled Toilets: Available in the Town End Terrace
Contact: (01205) 364406 (Bookings are necessary)

Travelling Supporters' Information:
From the North: Take the A17 from Sleaford, bear right after the railway crossing to the traffic lights over the bridge. Go forward through the traffic lights into York Street for the ground; From the South: Take the A16 from Spalding and turn right at the traffic lights over the bridge. Go forward through the next traffic lights into York Street for the ground.

BRACKLEY TOWN FC

Founded: 1890
Former Names: None
Nickname: 'Saints'
Ground: St. James Park, Churchill Way, Brackley, NN13 7EJ
Record Attendance: 2,604 (2012/13 season)

Colours: Red and White striped shirts with Red shorts
Telephone Nº: (01280) 704077
Ground Capacity: 3,500
Seating Capacity: 300
Web Site: www.brackleytownfc.com

GENERAL INFORMATION

Car Parking: At the ground (£2.00 charge per car)
Coach Parking: At the ground
Nearest Railway Station: King's Sutton (6¾ miles)
Club Shop: At the ground
Opening Times: Matchdays and by appointment only
Telephone Nº: (01280) 704077

GROUND INFORMATION

Away Supporters' Entrances & Sections:
No usual segregation

ADMISSION INFO (2014/2015 PRICES)

Adult Standing: £10.00
Adult Seating: £10.00
Senior Citizen/Student Standing: £5.00
Senior Citizen/Student Seating: £5.00
Under-16s Standing: £2.00
Under-16s Seating: £2.00

DISABLED INFORMATION

Wheelchairs: Accommodated
Helpers: Admitted
Prices: Normal prices apply for the disabled and helpers
Disabled Toilets: Available
Contact: (01280) 704077 (Stephen Toghill – bookings are necessary)

Travelling Supporters' Information:
Routes: From the West: Take the A422 to Brackley and take the first exit at the roundabout with the junction of the A43, heading north into Oxford Road. * Go straight on at the next roundabout and continue into Bridge Street before turning right into Churchill Way. The ground is located at the end of the road; From the South: Take the A43 northwards to Brackley. Take the second exit at the roundabout with the junction of the A422 and head into Oxford Road. Then as from * above; From the North-East: Take the A43 to Brackley. Upon reaching Brackley, take the 1st exit at the 1st roundabout, the 2nd exit at the next roundabout then the 3rd exit at the following roundabout into Oxford Road. Then as from * above.

BRADFORD PARK AVENUE FC

Founded: 1907   (Re-formed in 1988)
Former Names: None
Nickname: 'Avenue'
Ground: Horsfall Stadium, Cemetery Road, Bradford, BD6 2NG
Record Attendance: 2,100 (2003)
Pitch Size: 112 × 71 yards

Colours: Green & White striped shirts, White shorts
Telephone Nº: (01274) 604578 (Ground)
Office Address: Hugh House, Foundry Street, Brighouse   HD6 1LT
Office Number: (01484) 400007
Ground Capacity: 3,000   **Seating Capacity**: 1,247
Web site: www.bpafc.com

GENERAL INFORMATION
Car Parking: Street parking and some spaces at the ground
Coach Parking: At the ground
Nearest Railway Station: Bradford Interchange (3 miles)
Nearest Bus Station: Bradford Interchange (3 miles)
Club Shop: At the ground
Opening Times: Matchdays only
Telephone Nº: –

GROUND INFORMATION
Away Supporters' Entrances & Sections:
Segregation only used when required

ADMISSION INFO (2014/2015 PRICES)
Adult Standing/Seating: £11.00
Senior Citizen Standing/Seating: £7.00
Student Standing/Seating: £7.00
Under-16s Standing/Seating: Free of charge
Armed Forces Standing/Seating: Free of charge (warrant card must be shown)

DISABLED INFORMATION
Wheelchairs: Accommodated in front of the Stand
Helpers: Please phone the club for information
Prices: Please phone the club for information
Disabled Toilets: Available
Contact: –   (Bookings are not necessary)

Travelling Supporters' Information:
Routes: Exit the M62 at Junction 26 and take the M606 to its end. At the roundabout go along the A6036 (signposted Halifax) and pass Odsal Stadium on the left. At the roundabout by Osdal take the 3rd exit (still A6036 Halifax). After just under 1 mile, turn left at the Kinderhaven Nursery into Cemetery Road. The ground is 150 yards on the left.

CHORLEY FC

Founded: 1883
Former Names: None
Nickname: 'Magpies'
Ground: Victory Park Stadium, Duke Street, Chorley, PR7 3DU
Record Attendance: 9,679 (1931/32 season)
Pitch Size: 112 × 72 yards

Colours: Black & White striped shirts with Black shorts
Telephone Nº: (01257) 230007
Fax Number: (01257) 275662
Ground Capacity: 4,100
Seating Capacity: 900
Web site: www.chorleyfc.com
E-mail: info@chorleyfc.com

GENERAL INFORMATION
Car Parking: 80 spaces available at the ground
Coach Parking: At the ground
Nearest Railway Station: Chorley (¼ mile)
Nearest Bus Station: 15 minutes from the ground
Club Shop: At the ground
Opening Times: Matchdays only
Telephone Nº: –

GROUND INFORMATION
Away Supporters' Entrances & Sections:
Pilling Lane Stand entrances and accommodation

ADMISSION INFO (2014/2015 PRICES)
Adult Standing: £10.00
Adult Seating: £10.00
Concessionary Standing/Seating: £7.00
Under-16s Standing/Seating: £5.00
Under-12s Standing/Seating: £2.00
Under-8s Standing/Seating: Free of charge
Programme Price: £2.50

DISABLED INFORMATION
Wheelchairs: Accommodated by prior arrangement
Helpers: Please contact the club for information
Prices: Please contact the club for information
Disabled Toilets: Available in the Social Club
Contact: (01257) 230007   (Bookings are not necessary)

Travelling Supporters' Information:
Routes: Exit the M61 at Junction 6 and follow the A6 to Chorley. Going past the Yarrow Bridge Hotel on Bolton Road, turn left at the 1st set of traffic lights into Pilling Lane. Take the 1st right into Ashby Street and the ground is the 2nd entrance on the left; Alternative Route: Exit the M6 at Junction 27 and follow signs to Chorley. Turn left at the lights and continue down the A49 for 2½ miles before turning right onto B5251. On entering Chorley, turn right into Duke Street 200 yards past The Plough.

COLWYN BAY FC

Founded: 1885
Former Names: None
Nickname: 'Bay' 'Seagulls'
Ground: Llanelian Road, Old Colwyn, Colwyn Bay, LL29 8UN
Record Attendance: 2,400

Colours: Sky Blue shirts with Maroon shorts
Telephone Nº: (01492) 514680
Ground Capacity: 3,000
Seating Capacity: 500
Web site: www.colwynbayfc.co.uk

GENERAL INFORMATION

Car Parking: At the ground
Coach Parking: At the ground
Nearest Railway Station: Colwyn Bay (1 mile)
Nearest Bus Station: Colwyn Bay (Nº 23 stops at ground)
Club Shop: At the ground
Opening Times: Weekdays from 10.00am to 4.00pm
Telephone Nº: (01422) 514680

GROUND INFORMATION

Away Supporters' Entrances & Sections:
No usual segregation

ADMISSION INFO (2014/2015 PRICES)

Adult Standing/Seating: £11.00
Concessionary Standing/Seating: £7.00
Student Standing/Seating: £7.00
Under-16s Standing/Seating: £3.00

DISABLED INFORMATION

Wheelchairs: Accommodated in Covered Shelter
Helpers: Admitted
Prices: Normal prices apply
Disabled Toilets: Available in the Social Club
Contact: (01492) 514680 (Bookings are not necessary)

Travelling Supporters' Information:
Routes: From Queensferry: Take the A55 and when the expressway is reached take Junction 22 (signposted Old Colwyn). Turn left at the bottom of the slip road then straight on at the mini-roundabout into Llanelian Road. The ground is ½ mile on the right.

GAINSBOROUGH TRINITY FC

Founded: 1873
Former Names: None
Nickname: 'The Blues'
Ground: Northolme, Gainsborough, Lincolnshire, DN21 2QW
Record Attendance: 9,760 (1948)
Pitch Size: 111 × 71 yards

Colours: Blue shirts and shorts
Telephone Nº: (01427) 613295
Clubhouse Phone Nº: (01427) 613688
Fax Number: (01427) 613295
Ground Capacity: 4,340
Seating Capacity: 504
Web site: www.gainsboroughtrinity.com

GENERAL INFORMATION

Car Parking: Street parking and also in a Local Authority Car Park 150 yards from the ground towards the Town Centre
Coach Parking: Available by prior arrangement
Nearest Railway Station: Lea Road (2 miles)
Nearest Bus Station: Heaton Street (1 mile)
Club Shop: At the ground
Opening Times: Matchdays only
Telephone Nº: (01427) 611612

GROUND INFORMATION

Away Supporters' Entrances & Sections:
No usual segregation

ADMISSION INFO (2014/2015 PRICES)

Adult Standing: £12.00
Adult Seating: £13.00
Concessionary Standing: £8.00
Concessionary Seating: £9.00
Under-16s Standing/Seating: £4.00
Under-5s Standing/Seating: Free of charge

DISABLED INFORMATION

Wheelchairs: Accommodated
Helpers: Please phone the club for information
Prices: Normal prices for the disabled. Free for helpers
Disabled Toilets: Available in new block adjacent to the Main Stand
Contact: (01427) 613295   (Bookings are not necessary)

Travelling Supporters' Information:
Routes: From the North, South and West: Exit the A1 at Blyth services taking the 1st left through to Bawtry. In Bawtry, turn right at the traffic lights onto the A631 straight through to Gainsborough (approx. 11 miles). Go over the bridge to the second set of traffic lights and turn left onto the A159 (Scunthorpe Road). Follow the main road past Tesco on the right through the traffic lights. The ground is situated on right approximately a third of a mile north of the Town Centre; From the East: Take the A631 into Gainsborough and turn right onto the A159. Then as above.

GLOUCESTER CITY FC

Gloucester City are groundsharing with Cheltenham Town FC for the 2014/2015 season.

Founded: 1889 (**Re-formed**: 1980)
Forner Names: Gloucester YMCA
Nickname: 'The Tigers'
Ground: Abbey Business Stadium, Whaddon Road, Cheltenham, Gloucestershire   GL52 5NA
Ground Capacity: 7,136
Seating Capacity: 4,054

Record Attendance: 8,326 (1956)
Pitch Size: 110 × 72 yards
Colours: Yellow and Black Striped shirts, Black shorts
Telephone Nº: 07813 931781
Web Site: www.gloucestercityafc.com
E-mail: contact@gloucestercityafc.com

GENERAL INFORMATION
Car Parking: Available at the ground.
Coach Parking: At the ground
Nearest Railway Station: Cheltenham Spa (2½ miles)
Nearest Bus Station: Cheltenham Royal Well
Club Shop: At the ground
Opening Times: Matchdays only

GROUND INFORMATION
Away Supporters' Entrances & Sections:
No usual segregation

ADMISSION INFO (2014/2015 PRICES)
Adult Standing: £12.00
Adult Seating: £12.00
Under-18s Standing: Free of charge
Under-18s Seating: Free of charge
Concessionary Standing: £6.00
Concessionary Seating: £6.00

DISABLED INFORMATION
Wheelchairs: Accommodated in front of the Stagecoach West Stand (use main entrance) and in the In 2 Print Stand
Helpers: Admitted free of charge
Prices: Normal prices apply for disabled fans
Disabled Toilets: Available in the In 2 Print Stand, adjacent to the Stagecoach West Stand and in the Social Club
Contact: 07813 931781

Travelling Supporters' Information:
Routes: The ground is situated to the North-East of Cheltenham, 1 mile from the Town Centre off the B4632 (Prestbury Road) – Whaddon Road is to the East of the B4632 just North of Pittville Circus. Road signs in the vicinity indicate 'Whaddon Road/ Cheltenham Town FC'.

GUISELEY AFC

Founded: 1909
Former Names: None
Nickname: 'The Lions'
Ground: Nethermoor Park, Otley Road, Guiseley, Leeds   LS20 8BT
Record Attendance: 2,486 (1989/90)
Pitch Size: 110 × 69 yards

Colours: White shirts with Navy Blue shorts
Telephone Nº: (01943) 873223
Social Club Phone Nº: (01943) 872872
Fax Number: (01943) 873223
Ground Capacity: 3,000
Seating Capacity: 300
Web site: www.guiseleyafc.co.uk
E-mail: admin@guiseleyafc.co.uk

GENERAL INFORMATION

Car Parking: At the ground and in Netherfield Road
Coach Parking: At the ground
Nearest Railway Station: Guiseley (5 minute walk)
Nearest Bus Station: Bus Stop outside the ground
Club Shop: At the ground
Opening Times: Matchdays only
Telephone Nº: (01943) 879236 (weekdays)
Postal Sales: Yes

GROUND INFORMATION

Away Supporters' Entrances & Sections:
No usual segregation

ADMISSION INFO (2014/2015 PRICES)

Adult Standing: £12.00
Adult Seating: £12.00
Ages 12 to 16 Standing/Seating: £4.00
Under-12s Standing/Seating: Free of charge
Concessionary Standing: £7.00
Concessionary Seating: £7.00

DISABLED INFORMATION

Wheelchairs: Accommodated by the Players' Entrance
Helpers: Admitted
Prices: Free for both disabled fans and helpers
Disabled Toilets: None
Contact: (01943) 879236   (Bookings are advisable)

Travelling Supporters' Information:
Routes: Exit the M62 at Junction 28 and take the Leeds Ring Road to the roundabout at the junction of the A65 at Horsforth. Turn left onto the A65 and pass through Rawdon to Guiseley keeping Morrison's supermarket on your left. Pass straight through the traffic lights with the Station pub or your right and the ground is on the right after ¼ mile, adjacent to the cricket field.

HARROGATE TOWN FC

Founded: 1919
Former Names: Harrogate FC and Harrogate Hotspurs FC
Nickname: 'Town'
Ground: CNG Stadium, Wetherby Road, Harrogate, HG2 7SA
Record Attendance: 4,280 (1950)
Pitch Size: 107 × 72 yards

Colours: Yellow and Black striped shirts, Black shorts
Telephone Nº: (01423) 880675
Club Fax Number: (01423) 883671
Ground Capacity: 3,290
Seating Capacity: 502
Web site: www.harrogatetown.com
E-mail: enquiries@harrogatetown.com

GENERAL INFORMATION
Car Parking: Hospital Car Park adjacent
Coach Parking: At the ground
Nearest Railway Station: Harrogate (¾ mile)
Nearest Bus Station: Harrogate
Club Shop: At the ground
Opening Times: Monday to Friday 9.00am to 3.00pm and also on Matchdays
Telephone Nº: (01423) 885525

GROUND INFORMATION
Away Supporters' Entrances & Sections:
No usual segregation

ADMISSION INFO (2014/2015 PRICES)
Adult Standing: £12.00
Adult Seating: £12.00
Concessionary Standing/Seating: £7.00
Student Standing/Seating: £3.00
Under-16s Standing: £1.00 (when with a paying adult)
Under-16s Seating: £1.00 (when with a paying adult)
Note: Under-5s are admitted free of charge

DISABLED INFORMATION
Wheelchairs: Accommodated at the front of the Main Stand
Helpers: One helper admitted for each disabled fan
Prices: Free of charge for each disabled fan and helper
Disabled Toilets: Available
Contact: (01423) 880675 (Bookings are necessary)

Travelling Supporters' Information:
Routes: From the South: Take the A61 from Leeds and turn right at the roundabout onto the ring road (signposted York). After about 1¼ miles turn left at the next roundabout onto A661 Wetherby Road. The ground is situated ¾ mile on the right; From the West: Take the A59 straight into Wetherby Road from Empress Roundabout and the ground is on the left; From the East & North: Exit the A1(M) at Junction 47, take the A59 to Harrogate then follow the Southern bypass to Wetherby Road for the A661 Roundabout. Turn right towards Harrogate Town Centre and the ground is on the right after ¾ mile.

HEDNESFORD TOWN FC

Founded: 1880
Former Names: Formed by the amalgamation of West Hill FC and Hill Top FC
Nickname: 'The Pitmen'
Ground: Keys Park, Keys Park Road, Hednesford, Cannock   WS12 2DZ
Record Attendance: 4,412 (11th May 2013)

Colours: White shirts with Black shorts and socks
Telephone Nº: (01543) 422870
Fax Number: (01543) 428180
Ground Capacity: 6,039
Seating Capacity: 1,011
Pitch Size: 110 × 70 yards
Web site: www.hednesfordtownfc.com

GENERAL INFORMATION
Car Parking: 500 spaces available at the ground – £1.00 fee
Coach Parking: At the ground
Nearest Railway Station: Hednesford (1 mile)
Nearest Bus Station: Hednesford
Club Shop: At the ground
Opening Times: Matchdays and Weekdays from 10.00am to 4.00pm
Telephone Nº: (01543) 422870

GROUND INFORMATION
Away Supporters' Entrances & Sections:
No usual segregation

ADMISSION INFO (2014/2015 PRICES)
Adult Standing: £11.00
Adult Seating: £12.00
Concessionary Standing: £6.00
Concessionary Seating: £7.00
Note: A selection of family tickets are also available
Programme Price: £2.00

DISABLED INFORMATION
Wheelchairs: 8 spaces available in front of the Main Stand
Helpers: Please contact the club for details
Prices: Please contact the club for details
Disabled Toilets: 2 are available – one in the Main Building, one in the Hednesford End of the stand
Contact: (01543) 422870   (Bookings are necessary)

Travelling Supporters' Information:
Routes: Exit the M6 at Junction 11 or the M6 Toll T7 and follow signs for A460 (Rugeley). After crossing the A5 at Churchbridge Island, continue on the A460. After five traffic islands pick up signs for Hednesford Town FC/Keys Park and follow to the ground.

HYDE FC

Founded: 1885
Former Names: Hyde FC (1885-1917) and Hyde United FC (1917-2010)
Nickname: 'Tigers'
Ground: Ewen Fields, Walker Lane, Hyde, Cheshire, SK14 5PL
Record Attendance: 7,600 (vs Nelson, 1952)
Pitch Size: 114 × 70 yards

Colours: Red shirts with Black shorts
Telephone Nº: (0161) 367-7273
Fax Number: (0161) 367-7273
Ground Capacity: 4,073
Seating Capacity: 530
Web site: www.hydefc.co.uk
E-mail: secretary@hydefc.co.uk

GENERAL INFORMATION
Car Parking: 150 spaces available at the ground
Coach Parking: At the ground
Nearest Railway Station: Newton (¼ mile)
Nearest Bus Station: Hyde
Club Shop: At the ground
Opening Times: Matchdays only
Telephone Nº: (0161) 367-7273

GROUND INFORMATION
Away Supporters' Entrances & Sections:
No usual segregation although it is used as required.
When segregation is in operation, Away supporter enter the turnstiles behind the Social Club or in the Walker Stand, as directed.

ADMISSION INFO (2014/2015 PRICES)
Adult Standing: £13.00
Adult Seating: £15.00
Under-16s Standing: £5.00
Under-16s Seating: £7.00
Concessionary Standing: £8.00
Concessionary Seating: £10.00

DISABLED INFORMATION
Wheelchairs: Accommodated in the disabled area
Helpers: Please phone the club for further information
Prices: Please phone the club for further information
Disabled Toilets: Yes
Contact: (0161) 367-7273 (Bookings are not necessary)

Travelling Supporters' Information:
Routes: Exit the M60 at Junction 24 and then exit the M67 at Junction 3 for Hyde. Turn right at the top of the slip road, left at the lights (Morrisons on the left). Turn right at the next set of lights into Lumn Road then turn left at the Give Way sign into Walker Lane. Take the 2nd Car Park entrance near the Leisure Pool and follow the road round for the Stadium.

LEAMINGTON FC

Founded: 1891
Former Names: Leamington Town FC, Lockheed Borg & Beck FC, AP Leamington FC and Lockheed Leamington FC
Nickname: 'The Brakes'
Ground: New Windmill Ground, Harbury Lane, Whitnash, Leamington   CV33 9JR

Record Attendance: 1,380 (17th February 2007)
Colours: Gold and Black shirts with Black shorts
Telephone Nº: (01926) 430406
Fax Number: (01926) 430406
Ground Capacity: 5,000
Seating Capacity: 120
Web Site: www.leamingtonfc.co.uk

GENERAL INFORMATION
Car Parking: At the ground
Coach Parking: At the ground
Nearest Railway Station: Leamington (4 miles)
Club Shop: Please contact the club for information
Opening Times: –
Telephone Nº: –

GROUND INFORMATION
Away Supporters' Entrances & Sections:
No usual segregation

ADMISSION INFO (2014/2015 PRICES)
Adult Standing/Seating: £11.00
Concessionary Standing/Seating: £7.00
Under-16s Standing/Seating: £3.00 (Under-12s free)
Student Standing/Seating: £5.00

DISABLED INFORMATION
Wheelchairs: Accommodated
Helpers: Admitted
Prices: Normal prices apply for the disabled. Helpers are admitted free of charge
Disabled Toilets: Available
Contact: (01926) 430406   (Bookings are not necessary)

Travelling Supporters' Information:
Routes: Exit the M40 at Junction 14 and take the A452 towards Leamington continuing at the roundabout into Europa Way (still A452). After approximately ½ mile, take the 4th exit at the roundabout into Harbury Lane (signposted for Harbury and Bishops Tachbrook). Continue on Harbury lane, taking the 3rd exit at the first roundabout and going straight ahead at the traffic lights. The ground is on the left hand side of the road after approximately 1½ miles.

LOWESTOFT TOWN FC

Founded: 1880
Former Names: East Suffolk FC
Nickname: 'The Trawler Boys'
Ground: Crown Meadow, Love Road, Lowestoft, NR32 2PA
Record Attendance: 5,000 (1967)

Colours: Blue shirts and shorts
Telephone No: (01502) 573818
Ground Capacity: 3,000
Seating Capacity: 466
Web Site: www.lowestofttownfc.co.uk

GENERAL INFORMATION
Car Parking: Street parking only
Coach Parking: At Lowestoft College
Nearest Railway Station: Lowestoft (½ mile)
Club Shop: At the ground
Opening Times: Matchdays only 11.00am to 5.00pm
Telephone No: (01502) 567280

GROUND INFORMATION
Away Supporters' Entrances & Sections:
No usual segregation

ADMISSION INFO (2014/2015 PRICES)
Adult Standing: £12.00
Adult Seating: £12.00
Senior Citizen Standing: £9.00
Senior Citizen Seating: £9.00
Under-16s Standing: £3.00
Under-16s Seating: £3.00
Programme Price: £2.00

DISABLED INFORMATION
Wheelchairs: Accommodated
Helpers: Admitted
Prices: Concessionary prices apply for both the disabled and helpers
Disabled Toilets: Available
Contact: 07930 872947 (Bookings are necessary)

Travelling Supporters' Information:
Routes: Take the A146 or the A12 to Lowestoft Town Centre then head north on the A12 Katwijk Way Road. Turn left into Love Road for the ground.

NORTH FERRIBY UNITED FC

Founded: 1934
Former Names: None
Nickname: 'Villagers' or 'Green & Whites'
Ground: Eon Visual Media Stadium, Church Road, North Ferriby, East Yorkshire   HU14 3AB
Record Attendance: 2,232 (vs Hull City in 2013)
Pitch Size: 109 × 76 yards

Colours: White shirts with Green trim, Green shorts
Telephone Nº: (01482) 634601
Fax Number: (01482) 634601
Ground Capacity: 3,000
Seating Capacity: 500
Web site: www.northferribyunited.com
E-mail: info@northferribyunitedfc.co.uk

GENERAL INFORMATION

Car Parking: Limited spaces at the ground
Coach Parking: At the ground
Nearest Railway Station: Ferriby (5 minutes walk)
Nearest Bus Station: Hull
Club Shop: At the ground
Opening Times: Matchdays only
Telephone Nº: (01482) 634601

GROUND INFORMATION

Away Supporters' Entrances & Sections:
No usual segregation

ADMISSION INFO (2014/2015 PRICES)

Adult Standing: £12.00
Adult Seating: £12.00
Senior Citizen/Under-16s Standing: £6.00
Senior Citizen/Under-16s Seating: £6.00
Programme Price: £2.00

DISABLED INFORMATION

Wheelchairs: Accommodated
Helpers: Admitted
Prices: Standard prices apply
Disabled Toilets: Available
Contact: (01482) 634601   (Bookings are not necessary)

Travelling Supporters' Information:
Routes: North Ferriby is approximately 8 miles to the west of Hull on the A63. Upon reaching North Ferriby (from the West), proceed through the village past the Duke of Cumberland Hotel and turn right into Church Lane. The ground is situated on the left after half a mile.

OXFORD CITY FC

Founded: 1882
Former Names: None
Nickname: 'City'
Ground: Oxford City Stadium, Marsh Lane, Marston, Oxford   OX3 0NQ
Record Attendance: 9,500 (1950)

Colours: Blue & White hooped shirts with Blue shorts
Telephone Nº: (01865) 744493   or   07817 885396
Ground Capacity: 3,000
Seating Capacity: 300
Web Site: www.oxfordcityfc.co.uk
E-mail: ctoxford@btinternet.com

GENERAL INFORMATION
Car Parking: At the ground
Coach Parking: At the ground
Nearest Railway Station: Oxford (3¾ miles)
Club Shop: At the ground
Opening Times: Matchdays only
Telephone Nº: (01865) 744493

GROUND INFORMATION
Away Supporters' Entrances & Sections:
No usual segregation

ADMISSION INFO (2014/2015 PRICES)
Adult Standing: £11.00
Adult Seating: £11.00
Concessionary Standing: £6.00
Concessionary Seating: £6.00
Under-16s Standing: Free of charge
Under-16s Seating: Free of charge

DISABLED INFORMATION
Wheelchairs: Accommodated
Helpers: Admitted
Prices: Normal prices apply for the disabled and helpers
Disabled Toilets: Available
Contact: (01865) 744493   (Bookings are not necessary)

Travelling Supporters' Information:
Routes: The stadium is located by the side of the A40 Northern Bypass Road next to the Marston flyover junction to the north east of Oxford. Exit the A40 at the Marston junction and head into Marsh Lane (B4150). Take the first turn on the left into the OXSRAD Complex then turn immediately left again to follow the approach road to the stadium in the far corner of the site.

SOLIHULL MOORS FC

Photo courtesy of Jordan Martin Photography

Founded: 2007
Former Names: Formed by the merger of Solihull Borough FC and Moor Green FC in 2007
Nickname: 'The Moors'
Ground: The Autotech Stadium, Damson Park, Damson Parkway, Solihull B91 2PP
Record Attendance: 2,000 (vs Birmingham City)
Pitch Size: 114 × 76 yards

Colours: Yellow and Blue hooped shirts, Blue shorts
Telephone Nº: (0121) 705-6770
Fax Number: (0121) 711-4045
Ground Capacity: 3,300
Seating Capacity: 500
Web site: www.solihullmoorsfc.co.uk
E-mail: solihullfootball@btconnect.com

GENERAL INFORMATION

Car Parking: At the ground
Coach Parking: At the ground
Nearest Railway Station: Birmingham International (2 miles)
Nearest Bus Station: Birmingham (5 miles)
Club Shop: At the ground
Opening Times: Matchdays only
Telephone Nº: (0121) 705-6770

GROUND INFORMATION

Away Supporters' Entrances & Sections:
No usual segregation

ADMISSION INFO (2014/2015 PRICES)

Adult Standing: £9.00
Adult Seating: £9.00
Senior Citizen/Junior Standing: £5.00
Senior Citizen/Junior Seating: £5.00
Note: Under-12s are admitted free of charge when accompanied by a paying adult

DISABLED INFORMATION

Wheelchairs: Spaces for 3 wheelchairs are available
Helpers: Admitted
Prices: Normal prices apply
Disabled Toilets: Available
Contact: (0121) 705-6770

Travelling Supporters' Information:
Routes: Exit the M42 at Junction 6 and take the A45 for 2 miles towards Birmingham. Turn left at the traffic lights near the Posthouse Hotel into Damson Parkway (signposted for Landrover/Damsonwood). Continue to the roundabout and come back along the other carriageway to the ground which is situated on the left after about 150 yards.

STALYBRIDGE CELTIC FC

Founded: 1909
Former Names: None
Nickname: 'Celtic'
Ground: Bower Fold, Mottram Road, Stalybridge, Cheshire SK15 2RT
Record Attendance: 9,753 (1922/23)
Pitch Size: 109 × 70 yards

Colours: Blue shirts, White shorts and Blue socks
Telephone Nº: (0161) 338-2828
Daytime Phone Nº: (0161) 338-2828
Fax Number: (0161) 338-8256
Ground Capacity: 6,108 **Seating Capacity**: 1,155
Web site: www.stalybridgeceltic.co.uk
E-mail: office@stalybridgeceltic.co.uk

GENERAL INFORMATION

Car Parking: At the ground (£1.00 charge)
Coach Parking: At the ground
Nearest Railway Station: Stalybridge (1 mile)
Nearest Bus Station: Stalybridge town centre
Club Shop: At the ground and also at "Stitch in Time", Market Street, Stalybridge
Opening Times: Matchdays only at the ground Monday to Friday 9.00am to 5.00pm at Market Street
Telephone Nº: (0161) 338-2828

GROUND INFORMATION

Away Supporters' Entrances & Sections:
Lockwood & Greenwood Stand on the few occasions when segregation is required. No usual segregation

ADMISSION INFO (2014/2015 PRICES)

Adult Standing: £12.00
Adult Seating: £12.00
Concessionary Standing: £7.00
Concessionary Seating: £7.00
Note: Under-14s are admitted for £1.00 when accompanied by a paying adult

DISABLED INFORMATION

Wheelchairs: 20 spaces available each for home and away fans at the side of the Stepan Stand. A further 9 spaces available in the new Lord Tom Pendry Stand
Helpers: Please phone the club for information
Prices: Please phone the club for information
Disabled Toilets: Available at the rear of the Stepan Stand and at the side of the Lord Tom Pendry Stand
Contact: (0161) 338-2828 (Bookings are necessary)

Travelling Supporters' Information:
Routes: From the Midlands and South: Take the M6, M56, M60 and M67, leaving at the end of the motorway. Go across the roundabout to the traffic lights and turn left. The ground is approximately 2 miles on the left before the Hare & Hounds pub; From the North: Exit the M62 at Junction 18 onto the M60 singposted for Ashton-under-Lyne. Follow the M60 to Junction 24 and join the M67, then as from the Midlands and South.

STOCKPORT COUNTY FC

Founded: 1883
Former Names: Heaton Norris Rovers FC
Nickname: 'Hatters' 'County'
Ground: Edgeley Park, Hardcastle Road, Edgeley, Stockport SK3 9DD
Ground Capacity: 10,641 (All seats)
Record Attendance: 27,833 (11th February 1950)
Pitch Size: 111 × 72 yards

Colours: Blue shirts with White shorts
Telephone Nº: (0161) 2868888
Ticket Office: 0845 688-5799
Fax Number: (0161) 429-7392
Web Site: www.stockportcounty.com
E-mail: fans@stockportcounty.com

GENERAL INFORMATION
Car Parking: Booth Street (nearby) £4.00
Coach Parking: Booth Street (£20.00)
Nearest Railway Station: Stockport (5 minutes walk)
Nearest Bus Station: Mersey Square (10 minutes walk)
Club Shop: At the ground
Opening Times: Monday to Friday from 9.00am – 4.00pm. Open until 7.30pm on matchdays during the week and also on Saturday matchdays 10.00am – 2.45pm then for 30 minutes after the game.
Telephone Nº: (0161) 474-0310

GROUND INFORMATION
Away Supporters' Entrances & Sections:
Railway End turnstiles for Railway End or turnstiles for Popular Side depending on the opponents

ADMISSION INFO (2014/2015 PRICES)
Adult Seating: £15.00
Under-22s Seating: £10.00
Under-17s Seating: £3.00
Under-10s Seating: £1.00
Senior Citizen Seating: £10.00

DISABLED INFORMATION
Wheelchairs: 16 spaces in total. 10 in the Hardcastle Road Stand, 6 in the Cheadle Stand
Helpers: One helper admitted per disabled fan
Prices: £10.00 for the disabled. Helpers free of charge
Disabled Toilets: Yes
Contact: 0845 688-5799 (Bookings are necessary)

Travelling Supporters' Information:
Routes: From the North, South and West: Exit the M63 at Junction 11 and join the A560, following signs for Cheadle. After ¼ mile turn right into Edgeley Road and after 1 mile turn right into Caroline Street for the ground; From the East: Take the A6 or A560 into Stockport Town Centre and turn left into Greek Street. Take the 2nd exit into Mercian Way (from the roundabout) then turn left into Caroline Street – the ground is straight ahead.

TAMWORTH FC

Founded: 1933
Former Names: None
Nickname: 'The Lambs'
Ground: The Lamb Ground, Kettlebrook, Tamworth, B77 1AA
Record Attendance: 4,920 (3rd April 1948)
Pitch Size: 110 × 73 yards

Colours: Red shirts with Black shorts
Telephone Nº: (01827) 65798
Fax Number: (01827) 62236
Ground Capacity: 4,118
Seating Capacity: 520
Web site: www.thelambs.co.uk

GENERAL INFORMATION

Car Parking: 200 spaces available at the ground – £2.00 per car, £5.00 for per minibus or £10.00 per coach
Coach Parking: At the ground
Nearest Railway Station: Tamworth (½ mile)
Nearest Bus Station: Tamworth (½ mile)
Club Shop: At the ground
Opening Times: Weekdays from 10.00am to 4.00pm and also on Matchdays
Telephone Nº: (01827) 65798 Option 3

GROUND INFORMATION

Away Supporters' Entrances & Sections:
Gates 1 and 2 for Terracing, Gate 2A for seating

ADMISSION INFO (2014/2015 PRICES)

Adult Standing: £12.00 – £14.00
Adult Seating: £14.00 – £16.00
Under-16s Standing: £3.00 – £4.00 (Under-6s free)
Under-16s Seating: £5.00 – £6.00
Under-6s Seating: £3.00 – £5.00
Senior Citizen Standing: £7.00 – £9.00
Senior Citizen Seating: £9.00 – £11.00
Note: Prices vary depending on the category of the game.

DISABLED INFORMATION

Wheelchairs: Accommodated
Helpers: Admitted
Prices: Normal prices apply for Wheelchair disabled. Helpers are charged concessionary rates
Disabled Toilets: Yes
Contact: (01827) 65798 (Bookings are advisable)

Travelling Supporters' Information:
Routes: Exit the M42 at Junction 10 and take the A5/A51 to the town centre following signs for Town Centre/Snowdome. The follow signs for Kettlebrook and the ground is in Kettlebrook Road, 50 yards from the traffic island by the Railway Viaduct and the Snowdome. The ground is signposted from all major roads.

WORCESTER CITY FC

Worcester City FC are groundsharing with Kidderminster Harriers FC during the 2014/2015 season.

Founded: 1902
Former Names: Berwick Rangers FC
Nickname: 'The City'
Ground: Aggborough, Hoo Road, Kidderminster, Worcestershire   DY10 1NB
Ground Capacity: 6,444
Seating Capacity: 3,143
Record Attendance: 9,155 (1948)

Pitch Size: 110 × 72 yards
Colours: Blue and White shirts with Blue shorts
Office Address: Unit 7, Ball Mill Top Business Park, Hallow, Worcester   WR2 6LS
Telephone No: (01905) 23003
Fax Number: (01905) 26668
Web site: www.worcestercityfc.co.uk
E-mail: office@worcestercityfc.co.uk

GENERAL INFORMATION

Car Parking: At the ground
Coach Parking: As directed
Nearest Railway Station: Kidderminster
Nearest Bus Station: Kidderminster Town Centre
Club Shop: Online sales only at present
Telephone No: (01905) 23003

GROUND INFORMATION

Away Supporters' Entrances & Sections:
John Smiths Stand Entrance D and South Terrace Entrance E

ADMISSION INFO (2014/2015 PRICES)

Adult Standing/Seating: £13.00
Under-16s Standing/Seating: £3.00
Young Adult Standing/Seating: £6.00
Senior Citizen Standing/Seating: £9.00

DISABLED INFORMATION

Wheelchairs: Home fans accommodated at the front of the Main Stand, Away fans in front of the John Smiths Stand
Helpers: Admitted
Prices: Free of charge for both the disabled and helpers
Disabled Toilets: Available by the disabled area
Contact: (01905) 23003   (Bookings are necessary)

Travelling Supporters' Information:
Routes: Exit the M5 at Junction 3 and follow the A456 to Kidderminster. The ground is situated close by the Severn Valley Railway Station so follow the brown Steam Train signs and turn into Hoo Road about 200 yards downhill of the station. Follow the road along for ¼ mile and the ground is on the left.

THE FOOTBALL CONFERENCE SOUTH

Address

4th Floor, 20 Waterloo Street,
Birmingham   B2 5TB

Phone (0121) 643-3143

Web site   www.footballconference.co.uk

Clubs for the 2014/2015 Season

BASINGSTOKE TOWN FC

Founded: 1896
Former Names: None
Nickname: 'Dragons'
Ground: The Camrose Ground, Western Way, Basingstoke, Hants. RG22 6EZ
Record Attendance: 5,085 (25th November 1997)
Pitch Size: 110 × 70 yards

Colours: Yellow and Blue shirts with Blue shorts
Telephone Nº: (01256) 327575
Fax Number: (01256) 326346
Social Club Nº: (01256) 464353
Ground Capacity: 6,000
Seating Capacity: 650
Web site: www.basingstoketown.net
E-mail: richard.trodd@ntlworld.com

GENERAL INFORMATION

Car Parking: 600 spaces available at the ground (£1.00)
Coach Parking: Ample room available at ground
Nearest Railway Station: Basingstoke
Nearest Bus Station: Basingstoke Town Centre (2 miles)
Club Shop: The Camrose Shop
Opening Times: Matchdays only
Telephone Nº: (01256) 327575

GROUND INFORMATION

Away Supporters' Entrances & Sections:
No usual segregation

ADMISSION INFO (2014/2015 PRICES)

Adult Standing: £12.00
Adult Seating: £13.00
Concessionary Standing: £8.00
Concessionary Seating: £9.00
Under-16s Standing: £4.00
Under-16s Seating: £5.00
Under-11s Standing: £2.00
Under-11s Seating: £3.00

DISABLED INFORMATION

Wheelchairs: 6 spaces are available under cover
Helpers: Admitted
Prices: Normal prices for the disabled. Free for helpers
Disabled Toilets: Yes
Contact: (01256) 327575 (Bookings are not necessary)

Travelling Supporters' Information:
Routes: Exit the M3 at Junction 6 and take the 1st left at the Black Dam roundabout. At the next roundabout take the 2nd exit, then the 1st exit at the following roundabout and the 5th exit at the next roundabout. This takes you into Western Way and the ground is 50 yards on the right.

BATH CITY FC

Founded: 1889
Former Names: Bath AFC, Bath Railway FC and Bath Amateurs FC
Nickname: 'The Romans'
Ground: Twerton Park, Bath   BA2 1DB
Record Attendance: 18,020 (1960)
Pitch Size: 110 × 76 yards

Colours: Black and White striped shirts, Black shorts
Telephone Nº: (01225) 423087
Fax Number: (01225) 481391
Ground Capacity: 8,840
Seating Capacity: 1,026
Web site: www.bathcityfc.com
E-mail: info@bathcityfootballclub.co.uk

GENERAL INFORMATION
Car Parking: 150 spaces available at the ground
Coach Parking: Available at the ground
Nearest Railway Station: Oldfield Park (1 mile)
Nearest Bus Station: Avon Street, Bath
Club Shop: Yes – contact Andy Weeks, c/o Club
Opening Times: Matchdays and office hours
Telephone Nº: (01225) 313247

GROUND INFORMATION
Away Supporters' Entrances & Sections:
Turnstiles 17-19

ADMISSION INFO (2014/2015 PRICES)
Adult Standing: £12.00
Adult Seating: £13.00
Senior Citizen Standing: £8.00
Senior Citizen Seating: £9.00
Students/Under-18s Standing: £6.00 (**Under-16s** £3.00)
Students/Under-18s Seating: £7.00 (**Under-16s** £4.00)

DISABLED INFORMATION
Wheelchairs: 10 spaces available each for home and away fans in front of the Family Stand
Helpers: Admitted
Prices: Normal prices for the disabled. Free for helpers
Disabled Toilets: Available behind the Family Stand
Contact: (01225) 313247   (Bookings are necessary)

Travelling Supporters' Information:
Route: As a recommendation, avoid exiting the M4 at Junction 18 as the road from takes you through Bath City Centre. Instead, exit the M4 at Junction 19 onto the M32. Turn off the M32 at Junction 1 and follow the A4174 Bristol Ring Road south then join the A4 for Bath. On the A4, after passing through Saltford you will reach a roundabout shortly before entering Bath. Take the 2nd exit at this roundabout then follow the road before turning left into Newton Road at the bottom of the steep hill. The ground is then on the right hand side of the road.

BISHOP'S STORTFORD FC

Founded: 1874
Former Names: None
Nickname: 'Blues' 'Bishops'
Ground: Woodside Park, Dunmow Road,
Bishop's Stortford   CM23 5RG
Record Attendance: 3,555 (2000)
Pitch Size: 110 × 70 yards

Colours: Blue and White shirts with Blue shorts
Telephone Nº: (01279) 306456
Fax Number: (01279) 715621
Ground Capacity: 4,000
Seating Capacity: 500
Web site: www.bsfc.co.uk

GENERAL INFORMATION
Car Parking: 500 spaces available at the ground
Coach Parking: At the ground
Nearest Railway Station: Bishop's Stortford
Nearest Bus Station: Bishop's Stortford
Club Shop: At the ground
Opening Times: Matchdays only 1.30pm to 5.00pm
Telephone Nº: (01279) 306456

GROUND INFORMATION
Away Supporters' Entrances & Sections:
No usual segregation

ADMISSION INFO (2014/2015 PRICES)
Adult Standing/Seating: £12.00
Concessionary Standing/Seating: £7.00
Student Standing/Seating: £6.00
Under-16s Standing/Seating: £5.00
Note: Under-12s are admitted free of charge when
accompanied by a paying adult.

DISABLED INFORMATION
Wheelchairs: Accommodated in the disabled section
Helpers: Admitted
Prices: Free of charge for the disabled and helpers
Disabled Toilets: Yes
Contact: (01279) 306456   (Bookings are not necessary)

Travelling Supporters' Information:
Routes: Exit the M11 at junction 8 and take the A1250 towards Bishop Stortford. Turn left at the first roundabout and the ground is first right opposite the Golf Club (the entrance is between Industrial Units).

BOREHAM WOOD FC

Founded: 1948
Former Names: Boreham Rovers FC and Royal Retournez FC
Nickname: 'The Wood'
Ground: Meadow Park, Broughinge Road, Boreham Wood, Hertfordshire   WD6 5AL
Record Attendance: 4,030 (2002)
Pitch Size: 112 × 72 yards

Colours: White shirts with Black shorts
Telephone Nº: (0208) 953-5097
Fax Number: (0208) 207-7982
Ground Capacity: 4,239
Seating Capacity: 500
Web site: www.borehamwoodfootballclub.co.uk

GENERAL INFORMATION

Car Parking: At the ground
Coach Parking: At the ground
Nearest Railway Station: Elstree & Boreham Wood (1 mile)
Nearest Bus Station: Barnet
Club Shop: At the ground
Opening Times: 11.00am to 10.00pm Monday to Thursday; 11.00am to 6.00pm at weekends
Telephone Nº: (0208) 953-5097

GROUND INFORMATION

Away Supporters' Entrances & Sections:
No usual segregation

ADMISSION INFO (2014/2015 PRICES)

Adult Standing: £13.00
Adult Seating: £13.00
Under-12s Standing/Seating: £7.00
Under-17s Standing/Seating: £8.00
Senior Citizen Standing/Seating: £8.00

DISABLED INFORMATION

Wheelchairs: Accommodated
Helpers: Admitted
Prices: Concessionary prices are charged for the disabled and helpers
Disabled Toilets: None
Contact: (0208) 953-5097   (Bookings are necessary)

Travelling Supporters' Information:
Routes: Exit the M25 at Junction 23 and take the A1 South. After 2 miles, take the Boreham Wood exit onto the dual carriageway and go over the flyover following signs for Boreham Wood for 1 mile. Turn right at the Studio roundabout into Brook Road, then next right into Broughinge Road for the ground.

BROMLEY FC

Founded: 1892
Former Names: None
Nickname: 'Lillywhites'
Ground: The Stadium, Hayes Lane, Bromley, Kent, BR2 9EF
Record Attendance: 12,000 (24th September 1949)
Pitch Size: 112 × 72 yards

Colours: White shirts with Black shorts
Telephone Nº: (020) 8460-5291
Fax Number: (020) 8313-3992
Ground Capacity: 3,300
Seating Capacity: 1,300
Web site: www.bromleyfc.net
E-mail: info@bromleyfc.net

GENERAL INFORMATION

Car Parking: 300 spaces available at the ground
Coach Parking: At the ground
Nearest Railway Station: Bromley South (1 mile)
Nearest Bus Station: High Street, Bromley
Club Shop: At the ground
Opening Times: Matchdays only
Telephone Nº: (020) 8460-5291

GROUND INFORMATION

Away Supporters' Entrances & Sections:
No usual segregation

ADMISSION INFO (2014/2015 PRICES)

Adult Standing/Seating: £12.00
Concessionary Standing/Seating: £6.00
Under-16s/Student Standing/Seating: £5.00
Note: Under-5s are admitted free of charge

DISABLED INFORMATION

Wheelchairs: Accommodated
Helpers: Admitted
Prices: Please phone the club for information
Disabled Toilets: Yes
Contact: (0181) 460-5291 (Bookings are necessary)

Travelling Supporters' Information:
Routes: Exit the M25 at Junction 4 and follow the A21 for Bromley and London for approximately 4 miles before forking left onto the A232 signposted for Croydon/Sutton. At the second set of traffic lights turn right into Baston Road (B265) and follow for approximately 2 miles as it becomes Hayes Street and then Hayes Lane. The ground is on the right just after a mini-roundabout.

CHELMSFORD CITY FC

Founded: 1938
Former Names: Chelmsford FC
Nickname: 'City' or 'Clarets'
Ground: Melbourne Stadium, Salerno Way, Chelmsford CM1 2EH
Record Attendance: 16,807 (at previous ground)
Pitch Size: 109 × 70 yards

Colours: Claret and White shirts and shorts
Telephone Nº: (01245) 290959
Ground Capacity: 3,000
Seating Capacity: 1,400
Web site: www.chelmsfordcityfc.com

GENERAL INFORMATION

Car Parking: Limited space at ground and street parking
Coach Parking: Two spaces available at the ground subject to advance notice
Nearest Railway Station: Chelmsford (2 miles)
Nearest Bus Station: Chelmsford (2 miles)
Club Shop: At the ground
Opening Times: Matchdays only at present
Telephone Nº: (01245) 290959

GROUND INFORMATION

Away Supporters' Entrances & Sections:
No usual segregation

ADMISSION INFO (2014/2015 PRICES)

Adult Standing: £13.00
Adult Seating: £13.00
Under-16s Standing: £5.00
Under-16s Seating: £5.00
Under-12s Standing: Free of charge
Under-12s Seating: Free of charge
Concessionary Standing: £9.00
Concessionary Seating: £9.00

DISABLED INFORMATION

Wheelchairs: Spaces for 11 wheelchairs available
Helpers: Admitted free of charge
Prices: Disabled fans are charged standing admission prices
Disabled Toilets: Available
Contact: (01245) 290959 (Bookings are necessary)

Travelling Supporters' Information:
Route: The ground is situated next to the only set of high rise flats in Chelmsford which can therefore be used as a landmark. From the A12 from London: Exit the A12 at Junction 15 signposted for Chelmsford/Harlow/A414 and head towards Chelmsford along the dual-carriageway. At the third roundabout, immediately after passing the 'Superbowl' on the left, take the first exit into Westway, signposted for the Crematorium and Widford Industrial Estate. Continue along Westway which becomes Waterhouse Lane after the second set of traffic lights. At the next set of lights (at the gyratory system) take the first exit into Rainsford Road, signposted for Sawbridgeworth A1060. Continue along Rainsford Road then turn right into Chignal Road at the second set of traffic lights. Turn right again into Melbourne Avenue and Salerno Way is on the left at the end of the football pitches.

CONCORD RANGERS FC

Founded: 1967
Former Names: None
Nickname: 'The Beachboys'
Ground: Aspect Arena, Thames Road, Canvey Island, SS8 0HH
Record Attendance: 1,500

Colours: Yellow shirts with Blue shorts
Telephone Nº: (01268) 515750
Ground Capacity: 2,000
Seating Capacity: 340
Web Site: www.concordrangers.co.uk

GENERAL INFORMATION
Car Parking: At the ground
Coach Parking: At the ground
Nearest Railway Station: Benfleet
Club Shop: Available via the club's web site shortly
Opening Times: –
Telephone Nº: –

GROUND INFORMATION
Away Supporters' Entrances & Sections:
No usual segregation

ADMISSION INFO (2014/2015 PRICES)
Adult Standing: £10.00
Adult Seating: £10.00
Senior Citizen Standing: £5.00
Senior Citizen Seating: £5.00
Under-16s Standing/Seating: £3.00
Under-10s Standing/Seating: Free of charge

DISABLED INFORMATION
Wheelchairs: Accommodated
Helpers: Admitted
Prices: Normal prices apply for the disabled and helpers
Disabled Toilets: Available
Contact: (01268) 515750   (Bookings are necessary)

Travelling Supporters' Information:
Routes: Take the A13 to the A130 (Canvey Way) for Canvey Island. At the Benfleet roundabout, take the 3rd exit into Canvey Road and continue along through Charfleets Service Road into Long Road. Take the 5th turn on the right into Thorney Bay Road and Thames Road is the 3rd turn on the right. The ground is on the left-hand side by the oil storage tanks.

EASTBOURNE BOROUGH FC

Founded: 1963
Former Names: Langney Sports FC
Nickname: 'The Sports'
Ground: Langney Sports Club, Priory Lane,
Eastbourne   BN23 7QH
Record Attendance: 3,770 (5th November 2005)
Pitch Size: 115 × 72 yards

Colours: Red shirts with Black shorts
Telephone Nº: (01323) 766265
Fax Number: (01323) 741627
Ground Capacity: 4,400
Seating Capacity: 542
Web site: www.ebfc.co.uk

GENERAL INFORMATION

Car Parking: Around 400 spaces available at the ground
Coach Parking: At the ground
Nearest Railway Station: Pevensey & Westham (1½ miles but no public transport to the ground)
Nearest Bus Station: Eastbourne   (Service 6A to ground)
Club Shop: At the ground
Opening Times: Matchdays only
Telephone Nº: (01323) 766265

GROUND INFORMATION

Away Supporters' Entrances & Sections:
No usual segregation

ADMISSION INFO (2014/2015 PRICES)

Adult Standing: £12.00
Adult Seating: £12.00
Under-16s Standing: £1.00
Under-16s Seating: £1.00
Senior Citizen Standing: £8.00
Senior Citizen Seating: £8.00

DISABLED INFORMATION

Wheelchairs: 6 spaces available
Helpers: Admitted
Prices: Normal prices apply
Disabled Toilets: Available
Contact: (01323) 766265   (Bookings are necessary)

Travelling Supporters' Information:
Routes: From the North: Exit the A22 onto the Polegate bypass, signposted A27 Eastbourne, Hastings & Bexhill. *Take the 2nd exit at the next roundabout for Stone Cross and Westham (A22) then the first exit at the following roundabout signposted Stone Cross and Westham. Turn right after ½ mile into Friday Street (B2104). At the end of Friday Street, turn left at the double mini-roundabout into Hide Hollow (B2191), passing Eastbourne Crematorium on your right. Turn right at the roundabout into Priory Road, and Priory Lane is about 200 yards down the road on the left; Approaching on the A27 from Brighton: Turn left at the Polegate traffic lights then take 2nd exit at the large roundabout to join the bypass. Then as from *.

EBBSFLEET UNITED FC

Founded: 1946
Former Names: Gravesend & Northfleet United FC, Gravesend United FC and Northfleet United FC
Nickname: 'The Fleet'
Ground: Stonebridge Road, Northfleet, Gravesend, Kent   DA11 9GN
Record Attendance: 12,063 (1963)
Pitch Size: 112 × 72 yards

Colours: Reds shirts with White shorts
Telephone Nº: (01474) 533796
Fax Number: (01474) 324754
Ground Capacity: 5,258
Seating Capacity: 1,220
Web site: www.ebbsfleetunited.co.uk
E-mail: info@eufc.co.uk

GENERAL INFORMATION

Car Parking: Ebbsfleet International Car Park C (when available) and also street parking
Coach Parking: At the ground
Nearest Railway Station: Northfleet (5 minutes walk)
Nearest Bus Station: Bus Stop outside the ground
Club Shop: At the ground
Opening Times: Matchdays only
Telephone Nº: (01474) 533796

GROUND INFORMATION

Away Supporters' Entrances & Sections:
Only some games are segregated – contact club for details

ADMISSION INFO (2014/2015 PRICES)

Adult Standing: £10.00
Adult Seating: £10.00
Concessionary Standing: £8.00
Concessionary Seating: £8.00
Under-16s Standing/Seating: £5.00
Under-12s Standing/Seating: Free of charge

DISABLED INFORMATION

Wheelchairs: 6 spaces are available in the Disabled Area in front of the Main Stand
Helpers: Admitted free of charge
Prices: Please phone the club for information
Disabled Toilets: Available in the Main Stand
Contact: (01474) 533796   (Bookings are necessary)

Travelling Supporters' Information:
Routes: Take the A2 to the Northfleet/Southfleet exit and follow signs for Northfleet (B262). Go straight on at the first roundabout then take the 2nd exit at the 2nd roundabout into Thames Way and follow the football signs for the ground.

FARNBOROUGH FC

Founded: 1967   (Re-formed in 2007)
Former Names: Farnborough Town FC
Nickname: 'The Boro'
Ground: The Rushmoor Community Stadium,
Cherrywood Road, Farnborough   GU14 8UD
Record Attendance: 4,267 (15th May 2011)
Pitch Size: 115 × 77 yards

Colours: Yellow and Blue shirts and shorts
Telephone Nº: (01252) 541469
Fax Number: (01252) 372640
Ground Capacity: 4,190
Seating Capacity: 3,135
Web site: www.farnboroughfc.co.uk
E-mail contact: admin@farnboroughfc.co.uk

GENERAL INFORMATION

Car Parking: 260 spaces available at the ground with a further 200 spaces at the nearby Sixth Form college
Coach Parking: At the ground
Nearest Railway Stations: Farnborough (Main), Farnborough North, Frimley and Blackwater
Nearest Bus Station: Buses from Farnborough Main stop just outside the ground – please check the web site for details.
Club Shop: At the ground + web sales in the near future
Opening Times: Matchdays only
Telephone Nº: (01252) 541469

GROUND INFORMATION

Away Supporters' Entrances & Sections:
Moor Road entrances and accommodation

ADMISSION INFO (2014/2015 PRICES)

Adult Standing: £12.00
Adult Seating: £12.00
Concessionary Standing: £8.00
Concessionary Seating: £8.00
Under-16s Seating/Standing: £3.00
Under-6s Seating/Standing: Free of charge
Note: In keeping with F.A. Regulations, the Club reserves the right to charge higher prices for F.A. Trophy and F.A. Cup games.
Programme Price: £2.50

DISABLED INFORMATION

Wheelchairs: Spaces available in a disabled section in the PRE Stand
Helpers: Admitted free of charge
Prices: Concessionary prices charged for disabled fans
Disabled Toilets: Available in the PRE Stand
Contact: 0844 807-9900   (Bookings are not necessary)

Travelling Supporters' Information:
Routes: Exit the M3 at Junction 4 and take the A331 signposted for Farnham. After a few hundred yards exit at the second slip road – signposted A325 Farnborough – turn right at the roundabout and cross over the dual carriageway and a small roundabout. Pass the Farnborough Gate shopping centre on your left and at the next roundabout turn left onto the A325. Go over a pelican crossing and at the next set of lights take the right filter lane into Prospect Avenue. At the end of this road turn right at the roundabout into Cherrywood Road. The ground is on the right after ½ mile.

GOSPORT BOROUGH FC

Founded: 1944
Former Names: Gosport Borough Athletic FC
Nickname: 'The Boro'
Ground: Privett Park, Privett Road, Gosport, PO12 3SX
Record Attendance: 4,770 (1951)

Colours: Yellow shirts with Navy Blue shorts
Telephone Nº: (023) 9250-1042
Fax Number: (01329) 235961
Ground Capacity: 4,500
Seating Capacity: 450
Web Site: www.gosportboroughfc.co.uk

GENERAL INFORMATION

Car Parking: At the ground
Coach Parking: At the ground
Nearest Railway Station: Fareham (5½ miles)
Club Shop: At the ground
Opening Times: Matchdays only
Telephone Nº: –

GROUND INFORMATION

Away Supporters' Entrances & Sections:
No usual segregation

ADMISSION INFO (2014/2015 PRICES)

Adult Standing: £13.00
Adult Seating: £13.00
Concessionary Standing: £9.00
Concessionary Seating: £9.00
Under-19s Standing/Seating: £5.00
Note: Under-12s are admitted free of charge when accompanied by a paying adult

DISABLED INFORMATION

Wheelchairs: Accommodated
Helpers: Admitted
Prices: Normal prices apply for the disabled and helpers
Disabled Toilets: Available
Contact: (023) 9250-1042 (Bookings are not necessary)

Travelling Supporters' Information:
Routes: Exit the M27 at Junction 11 and follow take the A27 Eastern Way towards Gosport. Turn left at the roundabout to join the A32 Gosport Road and head south into Gosport. Continue along the A32 as it becomes Fareham Road then, at the second roundabout in a junction with two roundabouts, take the 3rd exit (signposted Alverstoke, Stokes Bay, Privett Park) into Military Road. Continue straight down this road, pass the playing fields on the left, then turn left at the roundabout into Privett Road. The entrance to the ground is the 4th turning on the left, just after the junction with Privett Place.

HAVANT & WATERLOOVILLE FC

Founded: 1998
Former Names: Formed by the amalgamation of Waterlooville FC and Havant Town FC
Nickname: 'The Hawks'
Ground: Westleigh Park, Martin Road, Havant, PO9 5TH
Record Attendance: 4,200 (2006/07)
Pitch Size: 112 × 76 yards

Colours: White shirts with Navy Blue rings, Blue shorts
Telephone Nº: (023) 9278-7822 (Ground)
Fax Number: (023) 9226-2367
Ground Capacity: 6,200
Seating Capacity: 665
Web site: www.havantandwaterloovillefc.co.uk

GENERAL INFORMATION
Car Parking: Space for 300 cars at the ground
Coach Parking: At the ground
Nearest Railway Station: Havant (1 mile)
Nearest Bus Station: Town Centre (1½ miles)
Club Shop: At the ground
Opening Times: Matchdays only
Telephone Nº: 07768 271143

GROUND INFORMATION
Away Supporters' Entrances & Sections:
Martin Road End

ADMISSION INFO (2014/2015 PRICES)
Adult Standing: £13.00
Adult Seating: £13.00
Senior Citizen Standing/Seating: £8.00
Concessionary Standing/Seating: £8.00
Note: When accompanied by a paying adult, children under the age of 11 are admitted free of charge

DISABLED INFORMATION
Wheelchairs: 16 spaces available in the Main Stand
Helpers: Admitted
Prices: Normal prices for disabled fans. Free for helpers
Disabled Toilets: Two available
Contact: (023) 9226-7822 (Bookings are necessary)

Travelling Supporters' Information:
Routes: From London or the North take the A27 from Chichester and exit at the B2149 turn-off for Havant. Take the 2nd exit off the dual carriageway into Bartons Road and then the 1st right into Martin Road for the ground; From the West: Take the M27 then the A27 to the Petersfield exit. Then as above.

HAYES & YEADING UNITED FC

Hayes & Yeading United FC are groundsharing with Maidenhead United FC during the 2014/2015 season.

Founded: 2007
Former Names: Formed by the amalgamation of Hayes FC and Yeading FC in 2007
Nickname: 'United'
Ground: York Road, Maidenhead, Berks. SL6 1SF
Pitch Size: 110 × 75 yards

Colours: Red Shirts with Black shorts
Telephone Nº: (020) 8753-2075
Fax Number: (020) 8753-0933
Ground Capacity: 4,500
Seating Capacity: 400
Web site: www.hyufc.com

GENERAL INFORMATION
Car Parking: Street parking
Coach Parking: Street parking
Nearest Railway Station: Maidenhead (¼ mile)
Nearest Bus Station: Maidenhead
Club Shop: None at present
Opening Times: –
Telephone Nº: –

GROUND INFORMATION
Away Supporters' Entrances & Sections:
No usual segregation

ADMISSION INFO (2014/2015 PRICES)
Adult Standing: £12.00
Adult Seating: £12.00
Concessionary Standing and Seating: £8.00
Under-18s Standing and Seating: £8.00
Under-16s Standing and Seating: £2.00

DISABLED INFORMATION
Wheelchairs: Accommodated
Helpers: Admitted
Prices: Normal prices for the disabled. Free for helpers
Disabled Toilets: Available
Contact: (01628) 636078   (Bookings are not necessary)

Travelling Supporters' Information:
Routes: Exit M4 at Junction 7 and take the A4 to Maidenhead. Cross the River Thames bridge and turn left at the 2nd roundabout passing through the traffic lights. York Road is first right and the ground is approximately 300 yards along on the left.

HEMEL HEMPSTEAD TOWN FC

Founded: 1885
Former Names: Apsley FC and Hemel Hempstead FC
Nickname: 'The Tudors'
Ground: Vauxhall Road, Adeyfield, Hemel Hempstead HP2 4HW
Record Attendance: 2,254 (vs Gosport Borough during the 2013/14 season)

Pitch Size: 112 × 72 yards
Colours: Shirts and Shorts are Red with White trim
Telephone Nº: (01442) 264300
Fax Number: (01442) 264322
Ground Capacity: 3,000
Seating Capacity: 350
Web site: www.hemelfc.com

GENERAL INFORMATION

Car Parking: At the ground
Coach Parking: At the ground
Nearest Railway Station: Hemel Hempstead (1½ miles)
Nearest Bus Station: Hemel Hempstead (¾ mile)
Club Shop: None

GROUND INFORMATION

Away Supporters' Entrances & Sections:
No usual segregation

ADMISSION INFO (2014/2015 PRICES)

Adult Standing: £10.00
Adult Seating: £10.00
Concessionary Standing/Seating: £6.00
Under-18s Standing/Seating: £3.00
Under-12s Standing/Seating: £1.00
Under-5s Standing/Seating: Free of charge
Programme Price: £2.00

DISABLED INFORMATION

Wheelchairs: Accommodated
Helpers: Admitted
Prices: Normal prices apply
Disabled Toilets: Available in the Clubhouse
Contact: (01442) 259777

Travelling Supporters' Information:
Routes: Exit the M1 at Junction 8 and go straight ahead at the first roundabout. When approaching the 2nd roundabout move into the right hand lane and, as you continue straight across be ready to turn right almost immediately through a gap in the central reservation. This turn-off is Leverstock Green Road and continue along this to the double mini-roundabout. At this roundabout turn left into Vauxhall Road and the ground is on the right at the next roundabout.

MAIDENHEAD UNITED FC

Founded: 1870
Former Names: None
Nickname: 'Magpies'
Ground: York Road, Maidenhead, Berks. SL6 1SF
Record Attendance: 7,920 (1936)
Pitch Size: 110 × 75 yards

Colours: Black and White striped shirts, Black shorts
Telephone Nº: (01628) 636314 (Club)
Contact Number: (01628) 636078
Ground Capacity: 4,500
Seating Capacity: 400
Web: www.pitchero.com/clubs/maidenheadunited/

GENERAL INFORMATION

Car Parking: Street parking
Coach Parking: Street parking
Nearest Railway Station: Maidenhead (¼ mile)
Nearest Bus Station: Maidenhead
Club Shop: At the ground
Opening Times: Matchdays only
Telephone Nº: (01628) 624739

GROUND INFORMATION

Away Supporters' Entrances & Sections:
No usual segregation

ADMISSION INFO (2014/2015 PRICES)

Adult Standing: £10.00
Adult Seating: £10.00
Concessionary Standing and Seating: £6.00
Under-18s Standing and Seating: £2.00
Note: Junior Magpies (Under-16s) are admitted free

DISABLED INFORMATION

Wheelchairs: Accommodated
Helpers: Admitted
Prices: Normal prices for the disabled. Free for helpers
Disabled Toilets: Available
Contact: (01628) 636078 (Bookings are not necessary)

Travelling Supporters' Information:
Routes: Exit M4 at Junction 7 and take the A4 to Maidenhead. Cross the River Thames bridge and turn left at the 2nd roundabout passing through the traffic lights. York Road is first right and the ground is approximately 300 yards along on the left.

STAINES TOWN FC

Photograph courtesy of Laurence Wakefield

Founded: 1892
Former Names: Staines FC, Staines Vale FC, Staines Albany FC, Staines Projectile FC & Staines Lagonda FC
Nickname: 'The Swans'
Ground: Wheatsheaf Park, Wheatsheaf Lane, Staines   TW18 2PD
Record Attendance: 2,860 (2007)
Pitch Size: 110 × 76 yards

Ground Capacity: 3,061
Seating Capacity: 500
Colours: Old Gold and Blue shirts with Blue shorts
Telephone Nº: (01784) 469240
Fax: (01784) 454735
Web site: www.stainestownfootballclub.co.uk

GENERAL INFORMATION
Car Parking: Large car park shared with The Thames Club
Coach Parking: At the ground
Nearest Railway Station: Staines (1 mile)
Nearest Bus Station: Staines Central (1 mile)
Club Shop: At the ground
Opening Times: Matchdays only
Telephone Nº: (01784) 463100

GROUND INFORMATION
Away Supporters' Entrances & Sections:
No usual segregation

ADMISSION INFO (2014/2015 PRICES)
Adult Standing: £12.00
Adult Seating: £12.00
Senior Citizen Standing/Seating: £6.00
Junior Standing/Seating: £5.00

DISABLED INFORMATION
Wheelchairs: Accommodated
Helpers: Admitted
Prices: Normal prices apply for the disabled. Free for helpers
Disabled Toilets: Available
Contact: (01784) 225943

Travelling Supporters' Information:
Routes: Exit the M25 at Junction 13 and take the A30 towards London. At the 'Crooked Billet' roundabout follow signs for Staines Town Centre. Pass under the bridge and bear left, passing the Elmsleigh Centre Car Parks and bear left at the next junction (opposite the Thames Lodge Hotel) into Laleham Road. Pass under the iron railway bridge by the river and continue along for ¾ mile. Turn right by the bollards into Wheatsheaf Lane and the ground is situated on the left by the Thames Club.

ST. ALBANS CITY FC

Founded: 1908
Former Names: None
Nickname: 'The Saints'
Ground: Clarence Park, York Road, St. Albans, Hertfordshire   AL1 4PL
Record Attendance: 9,757 (27th February 1926)
Pitch Size: 110 × 80 yards

Colours: Blue shirts with Yellow trim, Yellow shorts
Telephone Nº: (01727) 864296
Fax Number: (01727) 866235
Ground Capacity: 5,007
Seating Capacity: 667
Web site: www.sacfc.co.uk

GENERAL INFORMATION

Car Parking: Street parking
Coach Parking: In Clarence Park
Nearest Railway Station: St. Albans City (200 yds)
Club Shop: At the ground
Opening Times: Matchdays only
Telephone Nº: (01727) 864296

GROUND INFORMATION

Away Supporters' Entrances & Sections:
Hatfield Road End when matches are segregated

ADMISSION INFO (2014/2015 PRICES)

Adult Standing/Seating: £15.00
Concessionary Standing/Seating: £10.00
Under-12s Standing/Seating: £3.00
Note: One child under the age of 12 is admitted free with every paying adult.
Programme Price: £2.50

DISABLED INFORMATION

Wheelchairs: Accommodated
Helpers: One admitted per disabled supporter
Prices: Free for disabled, concessionary prices for helpers
Disabled Toilets: Available in the York Road End
Contact: (01727) 864296   (Bookings are not necessary)

Travelling Supporters' Information:
Routes: Take the M1 or M10 to the A405 North Orbital Road and at the roundabout at the start of the M10, go north on the A5183 (Watling Street). Turn right along St. Stephen's Hill and carry along into St. Albans. Continue up Holywell Hill, go through two sets of traffic lights and at the end of St. Peter's Street, take a right turn at the roundabout into Hatfield Road. Follow over the mini-roundabouts and at the second set of traffic lights turn left into Clarence Road and the ground is on the left. Park in Clarence Road and enter the ground via the Park or in York Road and use the entrance by the footbridge.

SUTTON UNITED FC

Founded: 1898
Former Names: Formed by the amalgamation of Sutton Guild Rovers FC and Sutton Association FC
Nickname: 'U's'
Ground: Borough Sports Ground, Gander Green Lane, Sutton, Surrey   SM1 2EY
Record Attendance: 14,000 (1970)

Colours: Shirts are Amber with a Chocolate pin-stripe, Amber shorts
Telephone N°: (020) 8644-4440
Fax Number: (020) 8644-5120
Ground Capacity: 5,013
Seating Capacity: 765
Web site: www.suttonunited.net

GENERAL INFORMATION
Car Parking: 150 spaces behind the Main Stand
Coach Parking: Space for 1 coach in the car park
Nearest Railway Station: West Sutton (adjacent)
Club Shop: At the ground
Opening Times: Matchdays only
Telephone N°: (020) 8644-4440

GROUND INFORMATION
Away Supporters' Entrances & Sections:
Collingwood Road entrances and accommodation

ADMISSION INFO (2014/2015 PRICES)
Adult Standing: £12.00
Adult Seating: £13.00
Child Standing: £2.00
Child Seating: £3.00
Senior Citizen Standing: £6.00
Senior Citizen Seating: £7.00

DISABLED INFORMATION
Wheelchairs: 8 spaces are available under cover accommodated on the track perimeter
Helpers: Admitted
Prices: Normal prices apply
Disabled Toilets: Available alongside the Standing Terrace
Contact: (020) 8644-4440   (Bookings are necessary)

Travelling Supporters' Information:
Routes: Exit the M25 at Junction 8 (Reigate Hill) and travel North on the A217 for approximately 8 miles. Cross the A232 then turn right at the traffic lights (past Goose & Granit Public House) into Gander Green Lane. The ground is 300 yards on the left; From London: Gander Green Lane crosses the Sutton bypass 1 mile south of Rose Hill Roundabout. Avoid Sutton Town Centre, especially on Saturdays.

WEALDSTONE FC

Photo courtesy of Steve Foster/Wealdstone FC

Founded: 1899
Former Names: None
Nickname: 'The Stones'
Ground: Grosvenor Vale, Ruislip   HA4 6JQ
Record Attendance: 1,638 (vs Rotherham United)
Colours: Royal Blue shirts with White shorts

Telephone Nº: 07790 038095
Fax Number: (020) 8930-7143
Correspondence Address: 31 Jersey Avenue, Stanmore   HA7 2JG
Ground Capacity: 3,000
Seating Capacity: 432
Web site: www.wealdstone-fc.com

GENERAL INFORMATION
Car Parking: 100 spaces available at the ground
Coach Parking: Available outside the ground
Nearest Mainline Station: West Ruislip (1 mile)
Nearest Tube Station: Ruislip (½ mile)
Club Shop: Yes
Opening Times: Orders through the post only
Telephone Nº: –

GROUND INFORMATION
Away Supporters' Entrances & Sections:
No usual segregation

ADMISSION INFO (2014/2015 PRICES)
Adult Standing: £12.00
Adult Seating: £12.00
Concessionary Standing: £7.00
Concessionary Seating: £7.00
Under-16s Standing/Seating: £2.00
Programme Price: £2.50

DISABLED INFORMATION
Wheelchairs: Accommodated
Helpers: Admitted
Prices: Normal prices apply
Disabled Toilets: Available
Contact: (01895) 637487

Travelling Supporters' Information:
Routes: Exit the M25 at Junction 16 and take the A40 towards Uxbridge. At the Polish War Memorial Junction with the A4180, follow the Ruislip signs (West End Road). After about 1½ miles, turn right into Grosvenor Vale for the ground.

WESTON-SUPER-MARE FC

Founded: 1899
Former Names: Christ Church Old Boys FC
Nickname: 'Seagulls'
Ground: Woodspring Stadium, Winterstoke Road, Weston-super-Mare   BS24 9AA
Record Attendance: 2,623   (vs Woking in F.A. Cup)
Pitch Size: 110 × 70 yards

Colours: White shirts with Black shorts
Telephone Nº: (01934) 621618
Fax Number: (01934) 622704
Ground Capacity: 3,071
Seating Capacity: 320
Web site: www.westonsmareafc.co.uk

GENERAL INFORMATION
Car Parking: 140 spaces available at the ground
Coach Parking: At the ground
Nearest Railway Station: Weston-super-Mare (1½ miles)
Nearest Bus Station: Weston-super-Mare (1½ miles)
Club Shop: At the ground
Opening Times: Matchdays only
Telephone Nº: (01934) 621618

GROUND INFORMATION
Away Supporters' Entrances & Sections:
No usual segregation

ADMISSION INFO (2014/2015 PRICES)
Adult Standing/Seating: £12.00
Senior Citizen Standing/Seating: £8.00
Students and Under-24s Standing/Seating: £8.00
Note: Under-10s are admitted for £1.00 when accompanied by a paying adult or senior citizen

DISABLED INFORMATION
Wheelchairs: Accommodated in a special disabled section
Helpers: Admitted
Prices: Normal prices apply
Disabled Toilets: Two available
Contact: (01934) 621618   (Bookings are not necessary)

Travelling Supporters' Information:
Routes: Exit the M5 at Junction 21 and follow the dual carriageway (A370) to the 4th roundabout (Asda Winterstoke). Turn left, go over the mini-roundabout and continue for 800 yards. The ground is on the right.

WHITEHAWK FC

Founded: 1945
Former Names: Whitehawk & Manor Farm Old Boys
Nickname: 'The Hawks'
Ground: The Enclosed Ground, East Brighton Park, Brighton   BN2 5TS
Record Attendance: 2,100 (1988/89 season)

Colours: Red shirts and shorts
Telephone Nº: (01273) 609736
Ground Capacity: 3,000
Seating Capacity: 200
Web Site: www.whitehawkfc.co.uk

GENERAL INFORMATION
Car Parking: At the ground
Coach Parking: At the ground
Nearest Railway Station: London Road (3¼ miles)
Club Shop: None
Opening Times: –
Telephone Nº: –

GROUND INFORMATION
Away Supporters' Entrances & Sections:
No usual segregation

ADMISSION INFO (2014/2015 PRICES)
Adult Standing: £10.00
Adult Seating: £10.00
Concessionary Standing: £5.00
Concessionary Seating: £5.00

DISABLED INFORMATION
Wheelchairs: Accommodated
Helpers: Admitted
Prices: Concessionary prices are charged for the disabled and helpers
Disabled Toilets: None
Contact: (01273) 609736   (Bookings are not necessary)

Travelling Supporters' Information:
Routes: Take the M23/A23 to the junction with the A27 on the outskirts of Brighton then follow the A27 towards Lewes. After passing Sussex University on the left, take the slip road onto the B2123 (signposted Falmer, Rottingdean) and continue for approximately 2 miles before turning right at the traffic lights into Warren Road by the Downs Hotel. Continue for approximately 1 mile then turn left at the traffic lights into Wilson Avenue. After 1¼ miles, turn left at the foot of the hill into East Brighton Park.

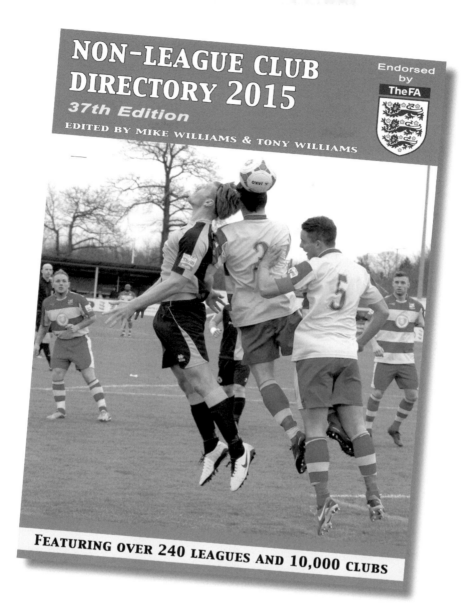

NON-LEAGUE CLUB DIRECTORY 2015

37th Edition

EDITED BY MIKE WILLIAMS & TONY WILLIAMS

Endorsed by The FA

FEATURING OVER 240 LEAGUES AND 10,000 CLUBS

Now in its 37th year of publication, The Directory has developed into a comprehensive record of competitions within the non-league game and gives this level of football the publicity and prestige it deserves.

The Football Association has encouraged the development of the publication since its introduction as a small pocket book in 1978 and all their competitions such as The Cup, Trophy and Vase plus their Youth and Women's cups are featured.

Individual club pages highlight the top twelve divisions with club details, records and statistics plus senior players are featured in team photographs and within many action shots from league and cup football.

Major competitions within the nation's pyramid of domestic leagues are featured from levels 1-7 with many leagues outside of the top seven steps featured also.

Football Conference National 2013/2014 Season	Aldershot Town	Alfreton Town	Barnet	Braintree Town	Cambridge United	Chester	Dartford	FC Halifax Town	Forest Green Rovers	Gateshead	Grimsby Town	Hereford United	Hyde	Kidderminster Harriers	Lincoln City	Luton Town	Macclesfield Town	Nuneaton Town	Salisbury City	Southport	Tamworth	Welling United	Woking	Wrexham
Aldershot Town		2-3	3-3	2-1	0-1	2-0	3-0	2-2	2-2	1-2	0-3	1-2	1-0	0-0	2-3	3-3	1-0	2-2	3-2	5-1	6-0	3-1	2-1	2-0
Alfreton Town	1-4		3-1	3-1	1-1	0-1	2-1	3-0	3-2	1-1	3-3	2-1	3-0	3-1	1-1	0-5	0-1	1-1	3-2	2-1	4-2	2-2	3-1	1-0
Barnet	1-3	1-0		1-1	2-2	3-0	1-0	0-4	2-1	0-1	2-1	2-0	3-2	1-0	1-1	1-2	1-2	1-1	3-1	1-0	1-0	0-0	1-3	1-1
Braintree Town	1-0	3-1	0-3		1-0	3-0	1-0	1-0	1-1	0-0	0-0	1-1	2-1	0-1	0-2	1-2	0-1	2-1	0-1	1-0	2-0	2-3	2-0	3-0
Cambridge United	4-0	0-1	1-1	1-0		0-1	1-1	5-1	2-1	1-0	1-2	1-0	7-2	5-1	1-0	1-1	3-0	3-0	2-0	3-1	3-0	2-1	2-0	0-0
Chester	1-1	0-1	2-1	0-2	0-0		0-0	2-1	1-2	1-1	0-0	3-2	0-0	3-3	1-1	2-1	3-3	2-2	2-2	2-0	1-3	0-2	0-0	
Dartford	1-1	1-0	0-2	0-2	3-3	0-1		1-2	0-1	0-1	1-0	2-0	4-3	3-0	1-2	1-2	1-2	1-1	1-0	2-3	1-2	5-1	1-5	
FC Halifax Town	4-0	2-0	2-1	0-0	1-1	2-1	2-0		1-0	3-3	4-0	1-1	4-0	1-1	5-1	2-0	2-1	2-2	5-1	1-0	2-0	3-0	3-4	3-2
Forest Green Rovers	3-1	3-1	1-2	0-2	3-2	3-0	1-0	2-1		1-0	2-1	1-1	8-0	1-1	4-1	0-0	2-3	1-0	4-0	3-1	1-2	0-0	2-2	1-1
Gateshead	0-0	3-0	1-2	1-0	2-0	3-2	2-0	1-1	1-1		1-2	2-1	4-0	3-1	3-1	0-0	2-2	2-1	3-2	2-2	5-0	1-1	0-2	0-3
Grimsby Town	1-1	3-1	2-1	1-0	0-1	2-1	5-2	0-1	3-1	2-2		1-1	1-0	3-1	1-1	1-2	2-3	1-2	2-0	0-0	3-1	1-1	2-2	3-1
Hereford United	0-2	3-2	0-1	1-1	1-0	2-2	2-2	3-2	1-0	0-1	0-1		0-0	1-1	1-0	0-0	2-1	0-1	1-0	4-1	1-0	2-1	0-2	0-2
Hyde	2-2	1-2	0-1	0-3	0-1	1-2	0-2	1-5	2-6	0-2	0-1	2-2		1-3	3-4	0-1	0-3	2-2	0-2	1-2	0-3	0-1	0-2	2-5
Kidderminster Harriers	0-0	1-3	1-0	2-2	2-0	3-1	1-2	2-0	4-1	3-1	0-1	2-1	2-1		4-1	0-2	2-1	0-0	3-0	1-1	5-3	2-0	2-0	3-1
Lincoln City	0-1	4-1	3-3	2-0	1-0	1-1	0-0	3-1	2-1	1-0	3-0	2-0				0-0	1-0	0-1	1-0	0-0	1-1	0-0	2-2	2-0
Luton Town	1-0	3-0	2-1	2-3	0-0	3-0	3-0	4-3	4-1	4-2	0-0	7-0	4-1	6-0	3-2		1-1	3-0	2-0	3-0	2-0	2-1	0-1	5-0
Macclesfield Town	1-1	0-1	2-0	0-1	0-1	3-2	3-1	2-2	1-2	0-2	1-1	1-0	3-0	1-1	3-1	1-2		0-1	1-0	2-2	2-1	2-1	3-2	3-2
Nuneaton Town	2-1	3-0	0-1	1-1	0-0	1-0	3-1	0-1	1-1	1-4	0-1	2-1	1-0	2-1	2-2	0-5	1-0		1-2	3-1	1-0	2-0	0-2	2-0
Salisbury City	1-0	0-0	2-1	1-1	0-3	3-1	1-0	3-1	1-4	0-0	1-0	4-1	2-0	1-1	1-2	0-0	3-2	2-1		1-1	0-1	3-0	2-0	2-1
Southport	1-0	2-1	1-1	0-4	1-0	0-0	3-0	2-1	2-0	2-1	2-1	0-3	1-1	1-2	0-1	1-0	4-1	1-0	3-1		2-0	2-2	1-1	1-2
Tamworth	1-0	1-0	0-0	0-0	0-1	3-4	0-2	2-0	1-2	0-1	0-2	1-0	1-1	0-3	0-0	3-4	1-0	1-1	1-2	4-1		1-1	2-4	2-2
Welling United	1-0	1-2	1-1	0-2	2-2	2-0	1-1	0-1	5-2	2-0	1-0	0-1	0-2	1-2	1-0	1-2	1-0	1-2	0-0	4-3	2-0		3-0	1-1
Woking	1-2	2-1	0-0	1-0	0-3	0-1	3-0	0-0	2-1	1-2	1-2	3-2	1-0	0-0	0-4	3-2	2-0	1-3	2-0	2-2	2-4			2-1
Wrexham	2-1	2-3	0-1	2-3	1-1	0-2	1-2	0-0	2-0	3-2	0-1	2-0	2-2	0-0	0-1	2-0	1-0	3-0	1-1	1-0	2-0	2-1	2-0	

Football Conference National

Season 2013/2014

Luton Town	46	30	11	5	102	35	101
Cambridge United	46	23	13	10	72	35	82
Gateshead	46	22	13	11	72	50	79
Grimsby Town	46	22	12	12	65	46	78
FC Halifax Town	46	22	11	13	85	58	77
Braintree Town	46	21	11	14	57	39	74
Kidderminster Harriers	46	20	12	14	66	59	72
Barnet	46	19	13	14	58	53	70
Woking	46	20	8	18	66	69	68
Forest Green Rovers	46	19	10	17	80	66	67
Alfreton Town	46	21	7	18	69	74	67
Salisbury City	46	19	10	17	58	63	67
Nuneaton Town	46	18	12	16	54	60	66
Lincoln City	46	17	14	15	60	59	65
Macclesfield Town	46	18	7	21	62	63	61
Welling United	46	16	12	18	59	61	60
Wrexham	46	16	11	19	61	61	59
Southport	46	14	11	21	53	71	53
Aldershot Town	46	16	13	17	69	62	51
Hereford United	46	13	12	21	44	63	51
Chester	46	12	15	19	49	70	51
Dartford	46	12	8	26	49	74	44
Tamworth	46	10	9	27	43	81	39
Hyde	46	1	7	38	38	119	10

Aldershot Town had 10 points deducted after entering administration.
Alfreton Town had 3 points deducted for fielding an ineligible player.
Salisbury City were demoted to the Conference South at the end of the season.
Hereford United were demoted to the Southern League Premier Division at the end of the season.

Promotion Play-offs

FC Halifax Town 1   Cambridge United 0
Grimsby Town 1   Gateshead 1

Cambridge United 2   FC Halifax Town 1
Cambridge United won 2-1 on aggregate
Gateshead 3   Grimsby Town 1
Gateshead won 4-2 on aggregate

Cambridge United 2   Gateshead 1

Promoted: Luton Town and Cambridge City
Relegated: Tamworth and Hyde

Football Conference North 2013/2014 Season	AFC Telford United	Altrincham	Barrow	Boston United	Brackley Town	Bradford Park Avenue	Colwyn Bay	Gainsborough Trinity	Gloucester City	Guiseley	Harrogate Town	Hednesford Town	Histon	Leamington	North Ferriby United	Oxford City	Solihull Moors	Stalybridge Celtic	Stockport County	Vauxhall Motors	Worcester City	Workington
AFC Telford United		3-1	0-1	2-1	2-1	2-1	4-1	3-0	2-1	4-2	0-1	5-3	3-2	1-2	2-0	4-0	1-1	3-1	2-0	1-0	0-0	2-1
Altrincham	1-1		2-1	0-0	1-0	4-1	3-1	3-0	2-0	4-1	1-3	1-3	2-2	3-2	1-1	2-2	1-0	5-0	3-0	5-1	1-2	2-0
Barrow	0-3	1-1		4-4	0-1	0-1	1-1	0-6	0-0	1-0	1-0	1-0	2-1	0-0	2-0	1-1	0-2	1-1	2-4	1-1	0-1	2-0
Boston United	1-1	3-2	1-0		1-2	2-3	2-1	6-0	2-0	3-0	3-3	4-0	0-0	2-0	2-0	2-1	4-1	4-1	0-0	5-2	2-1	5-3
Brackley Town	1-1	1-2	1-2	3-2		0-1	2-2	3-1	1-3	1-2	2-2	1-0	3-0	1-1	1-1	2-1	1-0	3-0	0-0	2-1	0-0	1-1
Bradford Park Avenue	3-1	2-4	2-2	1-1	0-5		1-2	4-0	3-1	0-3	0-0	1-2	3-0	3-2	0-4	3-3	2-2	1-1	0-2	0-0	6-1	1-0
Colwyn Bay	0-1	1-3	1-2	3-3	2-2	2-2		0-2	1-1	2-2	2-1	1-3	1-0	1-1	0-3	1-1	3-1	1-2	0-0	1-0	0-0	3-2
Gainsborough Trinity	1-3	5-4	2-1	0-1	2-2	4-2	0-2		3-3	1-2	2-0	1-2	3-1	1-1	1-4	6-0	2-3	0-2	1-5	1-1	2-1	3-0
Gloucester City	1-2	2-0	1-3	1-3	2-2	2-3	2-3	0-1		1-1	5-2	5-1	2-0	3-3	1-1	0-2	0-3	1-0	2-0	2-2	2-1	1-1
Guiseley	6-1	2-2	2-1	1-0	0-2	0-2	2-1	3-1	3-1		2-0	1-2	1-1	2-1	1-0	2-0	0-3	3-1	2-0	1-0	0-1	1-0
Harrogate Town	2-2	3-2	3-1	4-0	0-1	1-1	2-2	1-1	4-2	2-3		3-1	0-1	1-1	5-0	3-2	2-1	2-1	3-1	1-1	2-0	3-0
Hednesford Town	3-3	1-1	3-1	4-2	2-2	2-0	2-1	1-3	4-1	3-2	1-3		2-1	3-2	0-1	3-0	1-2	4-1	3-1	2-0	4-0	4-0
Histon	0-1	0-5	0-0	1-2	3-3	1-0	3-1	2-0	1-3	1-1	0-1	0-1		1-1	0-3	2-2	0-3	1-4	2-1	1-2	1-2	3-1
Leamington	2-2	0-1	1-1	0-0	3-1	2-0	2-1	0-1	0-1	2-3	1-2	2-1	1-0		0-2	4-0	0-1	1-0	2-1	0-1	1-0	2-0
North Ferriby United	2-2	2-1	2-2	3-0	1-1	2-1	2-3	2-0	3-1	2-3	3-2	3-0	4-4	4-1		2-1	1-1	2-0	0-0	2-0	2-1	3-1
Oxford City	2-0	1-2	0-1	1-1	0-0	1-1	1-2	1-0	1-0	3-3	1-2	1-2	2-1	2-2	2-3		0-2	2-1	4-1	3-0	0-0	1-1
Solihull Moors	2-2	0-1	0-2	1-2	1-0	2-2	2-2	3-2	2-1	3-0	2-3	0-0	0-0	2-0	2-2	2-2		3-3	1-0	1-0	1-1	1-1
Stalybridge Celtic	0-2	0-5	1-3	3-3	1-1	2-2	2-3	3-2	2-2	2-3	3-2	0-4	2-1	2-1	2-3	1-1	2-3		0-0	3-2	1-2	2-0
Stockport County	4-2	0-0	2-2	1-4	0-2	4-1	0-1	3-1	2-2	3-3	3-1	0-1	1-0	1-1	1-2	2-0	2-2	2-0		4-1	4-0	1-1
Vauxhall Motors	2-4	1-2	1-1	2-2	0-3	0-2	0-3	2-1	3-2	0-5	1-0	2-2	4-0	2-1	0-1	1-0	0-2	1-3	2-1		1-0	2-1
Worcester City	0-1	1-3	1-0	3-0	1-1	1-2	2-1	2-2	0-1	0-0	1-0	2-2	1-1	0-3	0-1	0-2	3-1	2-1	0-0	2-0		4-0
Workington	0-1	1-6	2-3	1-0	0-3	0-2	0-3	4-2	4-2	1-1	0-3	2-2	2-3	1-2	3-3	1-0	0-0	1-0	1-1	0-1	1-0	

Football Conference North

Season 2013/2014

AFC Telford United	42	25	10	7	82	53	85
North Ferriby United	42	24	10	8	80	51	82
Altrincham	42	24	9	9	95	51	81
Hednesford Town	42	24	6	12	87	65	78
Guiseley	42	23	9	10	78	56	78
Boston United	42	20	12	10	85	60	72
Brackley Town	42	18	15	9	66	45	69
Solihull Moors	42	17	14	11	63	52	65
Harrogate Town	42	19	9	14	75	59	63
Bradford Park Avenue	42	15	12	15	66	70	57
Barrow	42	14	14	14	50	56	56
Colwyn Bay	42	14	12	16	63	67	54
Leamington	42	13	13	16	54	53	52
Stockport County	42	12	14	16	58	57	50
Worcester City	42	13	11	18	40	53	50
Gainsborough Trinity	42	13	6	23	67	86	45
Gloucester City	42	11	11	20	64	77	44
Vauxhall Motors	42	12	8	22	43	74	44
Stalybridge Celtic	42	10	9	23	57	88	39
Oxford City	42	9	13	20	50	70	37
Histon	42	7	11	24	42	76	32
Workington	42	6	10	26	39	85	28

Harrogate Town had 3 points deducted for fielding an ineligible player. Oxford City had 3 points deducted for fielding an ineligible player. Vauxhall Motors resigned from the League at the end of the season.

Promotion Play-offs North

Guiseley 2   North Ferriby United 0
Hednesford Town 2   Altrincham 2

North Ferriby United 0   Guiseley 1
Guiseley won 3-0 on aggregate
Altrincham 2   Hednesford Town 1
Altrincham won 4-3 on aggregate

Altrincham 2   Guiseley 1

Promoted: AFC Telford United and Altrincham

Relegated: Histon and Workington

Football Conference South 2013/2014 Season

	Basingstoke Town	Bath City	Bishop's Stortford	Boreham Wood	Bromley	Chelmsford City	Concord Rangers	Dorchester Town	Dover Athletic	Eastbourne Borough	Eastleigh	Ebbsfleet United	Farnborough	Gosport Borough	Havant & Waterlooville	Hayes & Yeading United	Maidenhead United	Staines Town	Sutton United	Tonbridge Angels	Weston-super-Mare	Whitehawk
Basingstoke Town		0-0	0-0	1-0	0-1	2-3	0-1	2-1	2-0	1-2	2-0	2-2	4-0	2-1	0-1	0-1	2-2	2-1	0-1	0-0	3-2	1-3
Bath City	0-1		2-1	2-2	1-2	4-1	3-1	1-0	0-2	2-1	0-1	2-2	4-2	1-1	3-1	3-2	1-0	1-1	2-2	2-2	1-0	3-1
Bishop's Stortford	5-3	1-2		1-3	1-0	1-1	0-1	1-1	2-2	1-0	2-2	3-2	1-3	4-0	2-1	0-0	1-1	1-0	1-2	2-1	0-0	1-2
Boreham Wood	1-1	0-1	2-2		1-1	4-3	0-2	5-0	2-2	3-1	0-3	2-1	1-1	2-0	0-2	1-3	2-2	0-2	1-3	7-0	1-1	1-3
Bromley	3-2	2-2	3-2	2-1		5-0	1-2	4-1	0-4	2-1	1-2	0-0	3-0	2-1	2-0	2-1	6-1	3-0	2-4	5-1	2-1	4-0
Chelmsford City	1-0	1-0	2-1	0-6	3-1		2-2	4-1	0-4	3-0	0-0	1-2	3-1	1-0	0-0	0-0	0-3	3-2	0-2	7-1	1-2	0-2
Concord Rangers	1-2	0-2	0-2	0-4	2-3	1-3		1-0	1-2	1-1	3-2	1-2	5-0	0-2	3-4	3-1	4-1	2-1	0-0	2-2	2-0	1-1
Dorchester Town	0-4	0-2	1-3	1-4	3-2	2-0	2-2		0-4	0-0	1-2	1-3	1-0	1-1	0-2	0-2	0-3	1-1	0-0	2-1	0-3	2-6
Dover Athletic	1-1	2-0	2-3	0-0	0-2	2-2	0-1	1-0		0-0	1-2	2-1	0-1	3-0	0-0	0-1	2-0	1-0	0-1	3-1	1-2	1-1
Eastbourne Borough	1-3	3-2	4-1	1-0	1-1	4-2	0-0	0-1	0-4		1-1	1-1	5-2	1-3	0-1	3-1	2-0	2-0	1-1	2-1	2-0	0-2
Eastleigh	2-1	2-1	4-2	0-1	2-1	1-0	1-1	6-0	1-0	2-0		3-1	1-0	2-1	0-0	1-0	3-2	1-0	1-0	1-2	3-1	3-2
Ebbsfleet United	1-0	1-1	2-1	0-0	1-3	0-2	4-0	4-0	0-2	1-0	3-1		3-0	2-1	0-0	1-0	1-1	3-0	2-0	1-0	1-1	3-1
Farnborough	0-3	2-4	4-2	2-0	2-1	2-0	0-2	3-2	1-0	3-3	0-1	0-1		1-0	2-2	1-2	3-0	1-2	1-2	3-2	4-0	2-0
Gosport Borough	2-0	3-1	2-1	2-1	1-2	2-1	1-2	1-1	0-1	1-2	0-2	0-2	1-0		0-0	3-0	0-2	2-0	2-2	2-0	0-0	0-2
Havant & Waterlooville	4-1	1-0	2-0	1-1	1-0	3-0	1-0	5-1	3-4	1-1	1-0	1-0	2-1	3-0		1-2	1-3	0-2	0-5	1-2	2-0	2-0
Hayes & Yeading United	0-0	0-2	2-3	1-0	0-2	4-0	1-0	2-0	1-2	0-1	1-1	1-2	1-2	0-1	0-1		1-2	1-2	0-0	3-0	1-2	3-2
Maidenhead United	0-1	0-1	2-2	0-1	0-1	1-1	1-3	1-3	1-2	2-3	1-3	1-0	2-2	1-2	1-3	2-1		3-1	3-2	0-0	0-3	1-0
Staines Town	4-5	1-0	2-0	3-1	2-1	3-1	0-1	1-0	2-2	2-1	0-0	1-1	3-2	0-3	1-0	2-1	0-0		2-1	0-0	2-1	2-1
Sutton United	4-0	2-2	1-2	1-0	1-0	2-0	1-0	0-1	1-0	4-0	1-1	3-1	3-3	2-0	3-1	2-0	3-2	4-1		1-2	3-0	2-0
Tonbridge Angels	2-1	1-1	1-1	0-2	1-1	2-1	2-2	1-2	0-2	2-1	2-1	0-2	1-3	0-2	0-0	1-1	2-4	1-1	1-1		1-0	3-1
Weston-super-Mare	1-0	2-0	2-2	3-0	0-1	2-0	5-0	3-0	2-1	0-1	3-2	0-6	2-1	0-1	1-1	0-3	0-0	0-3	1-1	2-1		2-1
Whitehawk	1-0	2-2	1-1	0-2	1-2	0-4	0-2	3-0	0-1	1-2	1-4	1-1	3-1	1-1	2-2	1-0	0-3	3-3	3-3	1-0	0-0	

Football Conference South
Season 2013/2014

Eastleigh	42	26	8	8	71	40	86
Sutton United	42	23	12	7	77	39	81
Bromley	42	25	5	12	82	50	80
Ebbsfleet United	42	21	11	10	67	40	74
Dover Athletic	42	20	9	13	63	38	69
Havant & Waterlooville	42	19	12	11	57	43	69
Bath City	42	18	12	12	64	52	66
Staines Town	42	18	9	15	56	57	63
Concord Rangers	42	17	10	15	58	58	61
Eastbourne Borough	42	16	10	16	54	58	58
Weston-super-Mare	42	16	9	17	50	55	57
Gosport Borough	42	16	7	19	46	51	55
Boreham Wood	42	14	11	17	65	55	53
Basingstoke Town	42	15	8	19	55	56	53
Bishop's Stortford	42	13	13	16	63	68	52
Farnborough	42	16	4	22	62	77	52
Chelmsford City	42	14	7	21	57	77	49
Maidenhead United	42	12	10	20	55	69	46
Whitehawk	42	12	10	20	56	71	46
Hayes & Yeading United	42	13	6	23	45	52	45
Tonbridge Angels	42	9	13	20	43	77	40
Dorchester Town	42	8	7	27	33	94	31

Promotion Play-offs South

Dover Athletic 1   Sutton United 1
Ebbsfleet United 4   Bromley 0

Sutton United 0   Dover Athletic 3
Dover Athletic won 4-1 on aggregate
Bromley 1   Ebbsfleet United 0
Ebbsfleet United won 4-1 on aggregate

Ebbsfleet United 0   Dover Athletic 1

Promoted: Eastleigh and Dover Athletic

Relegated: Tonbridge Angels and Dorchester Town

The Evostik League Northern Premier League Premier Division 2013/2014 Season

	AFC Fylde	Ashton United	Barwell	Blyth Spartans	Buxton	Chorley	Droylsden	FC United of Manchester	Frickley Athletic	Grantham Town	Ilkeston	King's Lynn Town	Marine	Matlock Town	Nantwich Town	Rushall Olympic	Skelmersdale United	Stafford Rangers	Stamford	Stocksbridge Park Steels	Trafford	Whitby Town	Witton Albion	Worksop Town
AFC Fylde		1-0	1-0	5-1	2-2	0-1	5-0	0-2	2-0	1-2	1-2	1-0	0-0	2-0	1-2	2-1	2-3	2-1	2-0	5-0	2-1	3-1	3-0	3-2
Ashton United	1-1		0-1	3-3	2-0	2-1	4-1	2-1	2-2	2-1	1-3	5-1	4-1	0-0	1-0	2-0	4-1	4-0	2-1	3-2	2-0	3-4	1-4	2-3
Barwell	0-3	1-0		1-2	1-0	1-3	2-2	0-3	1-1	2-2	1-1	1-3	2-0	0-0	2-2	3-1	5-0	2-0	1-0	2-1	0-0	1-1	0-2	1-3
Blyth Spartans	1-1	2-1	2-1		0-1	3-1	3-0	0-1	2-0	2-1	3-2	1-3	2-2	1-2	2-2	3-2	2-1	6-2	2-1	3-0	2-1	0-7	4-2	3-3
Buxton	0-4	1-2	3-0	2-1		0-2	4-2	0-2	1-1	3-1	1-2	6-1	2-2	1-1	2-0	1-2	2-0	2-2	2-2	0-1	1-2	1-1	3-1	2-4
Chorley	3-1	3-3	1-2	3-0	0-0		13-1	0-1	2-0	3-1	2-1	1-0	4-0	3-1	5-1	0-1	4-1	3-0	3-0	3-1	6-2	0-0	1-0	1-0
Droylsden	0-10	0-9	1-2	0-0	1-1	0-5		1-4	2-3	0-3	1-5	1-2	0-4	1-4	1-6	1-5	0-3	2-3	0-3	2-3	0-6	0-2	4-3	3-4
FC United of Manchester	0-0	3-2	2-0	3-0	1-2	2-2	4-1		3-0	3-0	4-1	2-0	1-0	2-1	2-1	0-2	1-3	4-0	6-0	6-2	1-1	1-3	3-1	4-4
Frickley Athletic	0-2	0-2	2-1	0-1	0-1	0-0	2-0	1-2		3-2	0-1	2-2	1-1	1-3	2-0	4-2	4-3	2-0	1-1	2-2	2-1	1-1	0-0	2-2
Grantham Town	1-2	0-1	0-1	4-2	0-1	1-1	6-0	1-5	2-1		2-0	2-0	3-1	1-1	0-5	3-0	1-2	3-2	1-1	3-2	2-1	3-1	0-0	3-1
Ilkeston	0-1	1-2	4-2	0-1	0-2	2-3	5-1	3-3	1-0	0-2		3-4	1-2	1-3	3-1	0-1	2-1	0-0	3-0	6-1	1-1	0-2	1-1	0-0
King's Lynn Town	2-0	2-1	3-2	0-1	3-1	0-2	2-1	0-0	3-0	1-1	3-1		2-3	0-4	0-0	6-0	3-3	5-1	1-3	2-2	3-0	3-0	3-0	1-3
Marine	1-2	0-1	1-1	1-1	0-2	0-1	5-1	0-2	2-1	3-3	2-3	2-3		3-0	1-0	1-2	2-2	5-2	1-3	3-0	1-2	1-1	2-1	0-1
Matlock Town	1-1	0-0	2-1	1-1	1-2	2-0	1-1	0-0	4-1	1-0	2-0	0-0			2-1	1-1	2-1	0-2	2-0	3-0	3-2	2-0	0-1	1-0
Nantwich Town	1-1	2-2	2-0	1-1	1-1	1-2	4-0	1-1	2-1	1-1	2-2	2-0	1-2	1-1		3-2	2-2	4-1	3-1	2-1	0-1	4-3	0-2	2-3
Rushall Olympic	2-2	2-1	0-0	0-0	2-2	1-0	0-1	1-1	4-1	3-1	3-2	3-1	1-1	6-1	1-1		1-0	2-0	0-2	1-1	1-2	0-0	2-0	2-2
Skelmersdale United	0-5	1-1	1-0	4-3	2-0	1-0	7-3	1-3	3-2	1-2	2-0	3-0	4-1	1-0	2-1	1-0		3-2	0-1	6-0	3-1	4-2	1-3	2-1
Stafford Rangers	2-2	1-2	2-3	2-2	1-1	1-3	3-1	2-1	0-2	2-2	2-4	0-1	2-2	1-3	1-0	2-5	0-2		2-1	3-1	1-4	0-2	2-2	0-2
Stamford	1-3	2-1	0-2	3-4	1-0	1-1	4-0	2-3	6-4	1-2	0-2	3-0	2-4	1-0	2-2	3-4	2-0	2-0		4-3	2-2	1-2	3-1	2-2
Stocksbridge Park Steels	0-1	0-2	1-2	1-1	2-3	2-2	3-1	1-4	3-4	4-3	2-3	0-0	1-1	3-1	1-5	1-2	0-4	0-3	1-3		1-3	0-3	2-2	4-5
Trafford	2-0	4-1	2-4	2-1	0-0	0-5	1-0	2-3	4-1	2-1	2-5	1-2	1-0	2-1	0-1	3-1	2-0	1-2	0-2	1-0		0-3	3-3	0-2
Whitby Town	1-2	1-2	2-2	2-1	1-0	1-1	5-2	3-2	2-2	1-1	1-1	4-0	0-0	1-0	4-2	0-0	2-2	2-1	1-2	4-0	0-0		1-1	2-5
Witton Albion	0-1	1-2	1-2	0-1	0-1	2-2	5-1	2-5	2-1	2-1	2-1	1-0	2-3	1-0	3-2	2-4	2-3	5-0	2-1	4-1	0-4	3-1		2-2
Worksop Town	1-6	3-2	4-3	3-2	3-1	1-4	3-0	2-0	1-3	3-1	5-2	1-4	5-1	4-2	3-1	1-3	3-2	5-0	6-1	3-2	1-2	3-0	2-3	

Evo-Stik League – Northern Premier Division
Season 2013/2014

Chorley	46	29	10	7	107	39	97
FC United of Manchester	46	29	9	8	108	52	96
AFC Fylde	46	28	9	9	97	41	93
Worksop Town	46	27	7	12	120	87	88
Ashton United	46	24	8	14	92	62	80
Skelmersdale United	46	24	5	17	92	79	77
Rushall Olympic	46	21	12	13	79	65	75
Blyth Spartans	46	20	12	14	79	78	72
Whitby Town	46	18	16	12	82	64	70
Trafford	46	20	8	18	77	73	68
King's Lynn Town	46	20	8	18	76	77	68
Matlock Town	46	18	13	15	61	53	67
Buxton	46	16	14	16	63	60	62
Barwell	46	17	11	18	62	62	62
Grantham Town	46	17	10	19	77	78	61
Witton Albion	46	17	9	20	77	80	60
Ilkeston	46	17	8	21	81	77	59
Stamford	46	17	7	22	75	85	58
Nantwich Town	46	14	14	18	77	71	56
Marine	46	13	14	19	68	76	53
Frickley Athletic	46	12	13	21	62	80	49
Stafford Rangers	46	9	8	29	56	112	35
Stocksbridge Park Steels	46	5	8	33	60	130	23
Droylsden	46	2	3	41	40	182	9

Promotion Play-offs

AFC Fylde 3   Worksop Town 1
FC United of Manchester 1   Ashton United .... 2 (aet)

AFC Fylde 1   Ashton United .... 1 (aet)
AFC Fylde won 4-3 on aggregate

Promoted: Chorley and AFC Fylde

Relegated: Stafford Rangers, Stocksbridge Park Steels and Droylsden

Southern Football League Premier Division 2013/2014 Season

	AFC Totton	Arlesey Town	Banbury United	Bashley	Bedford Town	Bideford	Biggleswade Town	Burnham	Cambridge City	Chesham United	Chippenham Town	Corby Town	Frome Town	Hemel Hempstead Town	Hinckley United	Hitchin Town	Hungerford Town	Poole Town	Redditch United	St. Albans City	St. Neots Town	Stourbridge	Truro City	Weymouth
AFC Totton		2-2	1-3	3-1	1-1	2-2	1-5	2-1	3-2	0-2	3-1	2-1	0-5	1-4		0-5	1-3	3-1	0-3	2-5	2-2	1-4	2-3	0-1
Arlesey Town	2-2		2-1	0-1	3-0	1-1	3-2	2-2	0-2	3-2	1-0	1-1	1-2	2-3		0-0	5-2	2-2	0-3	2-3	1-1	1-5	1-1	2-3
Banbury United	3-4	3-2		3-3	3-0	1-0	6-4	2-2	1-5	0-4	2-0	3-1	1-2	0-3		2-1	0-7	0-0	2-0	1-5	0-1	0-4	1-2	0-0
Bashley	0-2	1-4	2-3		0-2	0-1	0-7	1-2	0-6	0-1	3-1	1-3	0-4	1-4		0-2	0-2	0-3	2-3	1-2	1-3	1-4	2-2	0-3
Bedford Town	3-2	0-2	2-0	0-1		2-4	1-5	3-3	0-4	0-3	0-3	2-4	0-2	0-3		0-1	1-4	1-5	1-2	2-2	1-2	2-0	0-1	0-3
Bideford	4-0	0-1	2-2	4-2	4-0		1-1	4-0	1-4	1-4	4-1	1-1	2-2	1-0		3-1	0-0	0-0	4-3	1-0	3-2	0-1	0-0	2-1
Biggleswade Town	1-1	2-1	1-2	0-0	4-1	3-0		1-1	1-2	3-2	3-3	0-1	2-0	5-2		3-2	0-1	2-2	0-0	0-0	2-2	2-2	2-1	2-1
Burnham	2-3	1-2	1-2	1-1	3-1	1-3	0-3		0-3	1-3	4-1	2-1	1-1	0-3		1-0	1-0	2-0	2-4	2-3	1-0	2-0	1-2	1-3
Cambridge City	3-0	2-1	3-1	7-1	1-0	1-1	1-1	7-2		1-2	2-1	1-0	2-0	1-1		3-2	0-0	1-2	4-1	0-3	3-2	2-1	4-1	4-2
Chesham United	4-1	3-3	8-0	4-1	3-0	2-2	2-1	1-2	3-0		2-0	2-1	2-1	1-3		1-2	1-0	0-2	3-1	1-0	3-0	0-1	4-2	0-0
Chippenham Town	1-2	0-1	2-0	2-0	1-4	2-4	1-3	2-1	1-0	0-3		0-0	3-3	0-3		2-0	2-3	1-2	3-0	1-1	2-1	0-9	3-1	2-1
Corby Town	3-1	1-3	4-2	3-1	2-0	3-0	1-1	0-3	0-2	2-1	2-2		0-1	0-2		1-2	0-3	2-3	2-0	1-0	3-4	3-2	3-1	
Frome Town	1-0	0-1	3-2	1-2	4-4	2-0	0-0	4-1	0-0	1-4	0-5	1-3		1-1		2-0	0-2	1-3	4-0	0-0	5-4	0-2	1-2	1-2
Hemel Hempstead Town	8-1	3-0	5-3	10-0	6-1	4-1	3-0	3-0	1-1	2-1	2-0	6-0	0-1			0-0	2-1	1-0	5-0	0-0	2-0	4-3	3-0	4-1
Hinckley United																								
Hitchin Town	1-1	1-0	5-0	1-0	6-1	0-1	1-0	1-1	1-0	1-2	3-1	0-2	1-2	2-0			0-2	2-2	0-2	1-1	4-0	1-1	2-3	3-2
Hungerford Town	4-0	3-0	3-1	3-1	2-0	2-1	1-1	2-3	3-2	0-1	1-1	1-2	0-0	0-4		2-3		2-0	0-2	3-1	1-0	1-0	6-0	2-1
Poole Town	2-0	5-3	4-1	5-0	1-3	3-3	2-1	0-0	0-1	1-0	3-1	3-1	4-2	0-2		1-0	0-0		2-1	2-1	2-0	1-2	1-0	2-2
Redditch United	2-1	1-3	2-3	4-0	2-0	3-1	2-2	2-1	4-1	1-2	3-0	1-3	1-0	1-0		1-0	0-5	0-2		1-3	0-0	1-6	3-1	0-4
St. Albans City	4-2	5-0	3-2	2-0	2-1	1-1	1-0	5-2	0-1	2-2	1-0	1-0	4-0	2-2		2-1	2-0	0-1	2-1		1-1	1-2	1-3	3-0
St. Neots Town	6-0	3-1	3-1	3-1	2-2	2-0	3-4	4-2	1-2	0-5	1-2	0-3	3-1	4-1		1-1	3-0	1-1	2-3	2-3		1-1	2-0	0-2
Stourbridge	3-0	0-2	5-0	4-1	2-1	0-3	2-1	1-0	3-2	2-3	0-1	3-1	7-0	1-4		1-1	1-2	5-2	5-1	0-1	2-1		2-2	7-0
Truro City	3-2	2-0	5-0	5-0	2-2	0-2	0-2	3-0	0-1	1-1	1-3	0-0	0-2	1-6		1-1	1-2	0-2	1-0	3-7	2-3	1-1		2-1
Weymouth	2-1	2-1	0-1	2-0	4-1	3-2	2-2	2-1	1-1	2-4	4-1	1-0	2-0	0-3		1-1	1-3	0-3	3-0	0-3	1-2	0-5	2-5	

The Calor League
Southern Premier Division

Season 2013/2014

Hemel Hempstead Town	44	32	6	6	128	38	102
Chesham United	44	29	5	10	102	47	92
Cambridge City	44	27	7	10	95	49	88
St. Albans City	44	25	10	9	89	49	85
Stourbridge	44	26	6	12	114	54	84
Hungerford Town	44	26	6	12	83	45	84
Poole Town	44	25	10	9	82	48	82
Bideford	44	18	13	13	75	64	67
Biggleswade Town	44	16	16	12	85	61	64
Redditch United	44	20	3	21	68	85	63
Corby Town	44	18	6	20	65	68	60
Weymouth	44	18	6	20	69	80	60
Hitchin Town	44	16	11	17	63	52	59
Frome Town	44	16	9	19	63	74	57
Arlesey Town	44	15	10	19	68	79	55
St Neots Town	44	15	9	20	74	76	54
Truro City	44	15	9	20	68	84	54
Chippenham Town	44	14	6	24	59	87	48
Banbury United	44	14	5	25	64	116	47
Burnham	44	12	8	24	60	91	44
AFC Totton	44	10	7	27	58	119	37
Bedford Town	44	6	6	32	46	114	24
Bashley	44	4	4	36	33	131	16

Poole Town had 3 points deducted for fielding an ineligible player.
Hinckley United folded on 7th October 2013 and their record was officially expunged from the league table on 21st October 2013

Promotion Play-offs

Chesham United	2	Stourbridge	1
Cambridge City	2	St. Albans City	4
Chesham United	1	St. Albans City	3

Promoted: Hemel Hempstead Town and St. Albans City

Relegated: AFC Totton, Bedford Town and Bashley

Ryman League Premier Division 2013/2014 Season

	AFC Hornchurch	Billericay Town	Bognor Regis Town	Bury Town	Canvey Island	Carshalton Athletic	Cray Wanderers	Dulwich Hamlet	East Thurrock United	Enfield Town	Grays Athletic	Hampton & Richmond Borough	Harrow Borough	Hendon	Kingstonian	Leiston	Lewes	Lowestoft Town	Maidstone United	Margate	Metropolitan Police	Thamesmead Town	Wealdstone	Wingate & Finchley
AFC Hornchurch	■	1-2	1-0	0-0	1-1	2-1	1-2	1-1	3-0	3-0	1-2	2-3	2-4	1-2	0-0	4-2	0-1	2-1	1-0	3-2	1-0	2-0	1-1	3-0
Billericay Town	2-2	■	1-2	0-0	1-4	3-1	1-2	2-0	0-1	0-2	4-0	1-2	2-1	0-1	3-2	4-1	0-1	0-1	3-3	0-2	1-2	3-2	4-2	1-0
Bognor Regis Town	1-1	1-0	■	5-2	5-0	2-4	4-0	4-2	3-1	5-1	0-3	4-0	3-2	3-0	0-0	0-0	3-1	4-1	1-2	5-3	2-0	2-1	1-3	1-0
Bury Town	3-2	0-1	2-0	■	0-1	0-1	1-0	0-4	0-0	3-3	2-1	0-0	3-2	0-4	0-3	0-2	2-1	1-2	1-2	1-1	2-1	0-0	0-1	2-0
Canvey Island	1-1	1-2	1-3	0-2	■	3-2	4-0	2-1	2-1	2-1	1-0	2-1	1-3	0-0	0-1	2-3	3-3	0-0	0-1	2-0	1-1	2-2	3-2	2-0
Carshalton Athletic	0-1	1-0	1-3	1-3	1-1	■	0-2	0-4	1-2	1-4	1-1	2-0	1-2	0-2	1-3	0-1	1-0	0-1	1-2	0-6	1-1	0-4	2-4	0-4
Cray Wanderers	1-6	0-1	1-2	1-3	2-1	0-0	■	0-6	1-3	1-2	3-2	1-1	0-1	0-6	0-4	2-2	1-5	0-4	0-5	1-4	4-1	3-4	0-3	2-2
Dulwich Hamlet	2-3	2-1	0-2	1-0	1-0	3-1	4-0	■	3-0	2-2	3-2	2-2	3-2	2-0	1-1	2-3	4-2	2-0	2-0	2-0	1-2	2-0	1-4	4-2
East Thurrock United	1-2	2-2	4-2	2-2	2-0	2-3	3-0	1-4	■	1-1	3-0	0-1	1-3	6-1	2-0	1-2	0-2	0-1	3-1	1-4	1-1	3-1	0-3	0-1
Enfield Town	0-2	1-2	2-1	1-0	3-3	2-2	1-0	3-4	3-5	■	1-1	3-0	1-0	3-2	0-1	1-3	2-1	2-2	1-1	1-1	2-1	3-1	2-4	0-3
Grays Athletic	1-5	2-2	3-4	4-3	1-4	1-4	3-0	0-0	2-0	2-0	■	1-3	2-0	1-3	0-0	3-2	4-2	1-1	0-1	3-0	0-0	1-4	1-1	2-0
Hampton & Richmond Borough	1-1	0-1	4-3	3-0	0-2	4-0	4-0	0-1	1-0	2-0	0-2	■	1-1	5-2	4-1	0-2	1-1	1-2	1-3	1-2	1-3	0-1	0-3	0-2
Harrow Borough	1-2	1-1	0-0	0-2	2-0	4-2	3-1	2-2	1-1	2-2	3-2	0-2	■	1-3	0-0	1-1	2-0	1-1	4-1	0-0	1-2	1-2	0-2	0-2
Hendon	0-1	1-2	1-0	1-0	4-2	1-0	2-0	1-2	2-2	0-3	2-3	3-4	1-2	■	1-2	3-1	1-1	0-1	3-5	2-3	4-1	5-2	0-0	1-1
Kingstonian	1-1	0-2	1-2	2-1	3-1	5-1	4-0	2-1	3-0	3-0	4-1	1-0	2-2	1-4	■	2-0	4-1	1-0	0-3	2-0	1-2	4-1	0-1	1-0
Leiston	2-3	2-2	5-2	0-4	0-2	0-1	4-1	2-1	3-1	6-1	4-1	0-0	0-1	1-0	0-0	■	2-2	1-0	1-0	1-1	3-0	0-2	0-2	0-2
Lewes	1-5	1-1	1-1	1-4	1-0	2-0	4-2	2-0	2-2	3-1	0-1	1-1	1-1	0-2	1-1	5-1	■	0-2	1-0	3-0	2-2	1-1	0-3	3-0
Lowestoft Town	3-0	1-0	2-0	1-3	2-1	5-0	0-2	2-0	3-0	2-0	2-2	0-3	3-0	2-3	2-0	3-0	1-1	■	2-1	3-0	1-1	5-0	1-1	7-0
Maidstone United	1-1	2-1	1-2	1-1	1-1	1-0	3-0	4-3	1-1	3-0	2-1	7-2	4-4	1-1	2-0	2-2	0-0	2-0	■	4-0	1-1	4-0	1-1	5-0
Margate	1-2	1-2	1-1	1-2	1-0	5-0	2-4	1-1	1-0	2-5	2-2	3-1	2-3	1-2	1-1	1-1	3-0	1-0	1-3	■	1-0	2-1	0-1	3-2
Metropolitan Police	2-1	0-2	0-2	0-3	0-1	3-0	7-1	0-0	1-2	3-1	1-2	1-3	2-0	0-1	0-2	2-1	0-0	0-0	1-2	0-2	■	3-1	2-1	3-1
Thamesmead Town	1-2	3-3	1-2	4-2	2-0	1-1	2-1	1-3	1-0	1-1	1-0	1-1	0-1	0-4	2-2	2-4	2-0	2-2	4-1	0-2	0-0	■	0-2	1-2
Wealdstone	2-0	2-0	2-2	3-0	2-0	3-1	7-1	2-2	5-0	4-1	3-1	1-3	3-0	1-1	0-4	3-1	2-2	0-0	2-1	0-1	1-1	2-0	■	2-2
Wingate & Finchley	0-3	5-0	3-0	1-0	0-4	4-0	1-1	2-3	4-3	1-1	1-3	1-2	3-1	1-0	0-4	0-1	1-3	0-0	2-4	0-0	0-3	3-1	0-2	■

Ryman League Premier Division

Season 2013/2014

	P	W	D	L	F	A	Pts
Wealdstone	46	28	12	6	99	43	96
Kingstonian	46	25	10	11	80	44	85
Bognor Regis Town	46	26	7	13	95	65	85
Lowestoft Town	46	24	12	10	76	40	84
AFC Hornchurch	46	24	11	11	83	53	83
Dulwich Hamlet	46	25	7	14	96	65	82
Maidstone United	46	23	12	11	92	57	81
Hendon	46	21	7	18	84	69	70
Leiston	46	19	10	17	73	71	67
Billericay Town	46	19	9	18	66	64	66
Margate	46	18	10	18	70	67	64
Hampton & Richmond Borough	46	18	10	18	72	70	64
Canvey Island	46	17	11	18	65	65	62
Grays Athletic	46	17	10	19	74	82	61
Bury Town	46	17	9	20	60	65	60
Lewes	46	14	17	15	67	67	59
Metropolitan Police	46	15	13	18	58	59	58
Harrow Borough	46	15	13	18	66	72	58
Enfield Town	46	13	12	21	64	90	51
East Thurrock United	46	13	10	23	66	84	49
Wingate & Finchley	46	14	7	25	57	84	49
Thamesmead Town	46	12	10	24	61	90	46
Carshalton Athletic	46	8	6	32	40	101	30
Cray Wanderers	46	7	5	34	40	138	26

Promotion Play-offs

Kingstonian 0   AFC Hornchurch 1
Bognor Regis Town 1   Lowestoft Town 2

Lowestoft Town 3   AFC Hornchurch 0

Promoted: Wealdstone and Lowestoft Town

Relegated: Thamesmead Town, Carshalton Athletic and Cray Wanderers

F.A. Trophy 2013/2014

Qualifying 1	AFC Fylde	1	Kendal Town	1
Qualifying 1	AFC Sudbury	5	Crawley Down Gatwick	0
Qualifying 1	AFC Totton	1	Clevedon Town	2
Qualifying 1	Arlesey Town	3	Waltham Abbey	0
Qualifying 1	Ashton United	0	Sheffield	3
Qualifying 1	Aylesbury United	0	Ramsgate	1
Qualifying 1	Barwell	0	Rushall Olympic	4
Qualifying 1	Belper Town	2	Mickleover Sports	3
Qualifying 1	Biggleswade Town	0	Chesham United	1
Qualifying 1	Blyth Spartans	6	Skelmersdale United	0
Qualifying 1	Bognor Regis Town	2	Thurrock	1
Qualifying 1	Burnham	2	Paulton Rovers	1
Qualifying 1	Burnham Ramblers	0	Carshalton Athletic	1
Qualifying 1	Bury Town	2	Dereham Town	0
Qualifying 1	Buxton	1	Darlington 1883	1
Qualifying 1	Cammell Laird	0	Curzon Ashton	1
Qualifying 1	Chatham Town	2	AFC Hayes	0
Qualifying 1	Cheshunt	3	Three Bridges	4
Qualifying 1	Chippenham Town	3	Chertsey Town	0
Qualifying 1	Coalville Town	3	Stafford Rangers	2
Qualifying 1	Cray Wanderers	1	Hendon	4
Qualifying 1	Daventry Town	2	Corby Town	1
Qualifying 1	Droylsden	0	Nantwich Town	3
Qualifying 1	Dulwich Hamlet	2	Harrow Borough	1
Qualifying 1	Dunstable Town	3	Peacehaven & Telscombe	2
Qualifying 1	Eastbourne Town	0	East Thurrock United	0
Qualifying 1	Egham Town	3	Cirencester Town	2
Qualifying 1	Enfield Town	2	Lowestoft Town	1
Qualifying 1	Evesham United	0	Leek Town	2
Qualifying 1	Folkestone Invicta	2	Kingstonian	0
Qualifying 1	Frickley Athletic	1	Brigg Town	2
Qualifying 1	Frome Town	1	Poole Town	1
Qualifying 1	Grantham Town	2	Soham Town Rangers	2
Qualifying 1	Grays Athletic	1	Herne Bay	1
Qualifying 1	Gresley	2	Ilkeston	1
Qualifying 1	Guernsey	1	Billericay Town	2
Qualifying 1	Halesowen Town	1	St. Neots Town	3
Qualifying 1	Hampton & Richmond Borough	1	Bedford Town	1
Qualifying 1	Hastings United	4	Horsham	2
Qualifying 1	Hemel Hempstead Town	3	AFC Hornchurch	2
Qualifying 1	Heybridge Swifts	1	Canvey Island	2
Qualifying 1	Hungerford Town	4	Bashley	2
Qualifying 1	Hythe Town	3	Tilbury	1
Qualifying 1	Kettering Town	0	St. Ives Town	1
Qualifying 1	King's Lynn Town	1	Cambridge City	2
Qualifying 1	Leiston	0	Wealdstone	3
Qualifying 1	Lewes	1	Leatherhead	2
Qualifying 1	Maldon & Tiptree	1	Maidstone United	3
Qualifying 1	Marine	1	Burscough	1
Qualifying 1	Marlow	4	North Leigh	1
Qualifying 1	Matlock Town	–	Hinckley United	–
	Walkover for Matlock Town after Hinckley United were expelled from the competition.			
Qualifying 1	Mossley	3	Lancaster City	2
Qualifying 1	North Greenford United	2	Aylesbury	1
Qualifying 1	Northwich Victoria	2	Radcliffe Borough	0

Qualifying 1	Ramsbottom United	7	Worksop Town	2	
Qualifying 1	Redditch United	2	Chasetown	0	
Qualifying 1	Shortwood United	0	Mangotsfield United	2	
Qualifying 1	Slough Town	1	Merthyr Town	2	
Qualifying 1	Stamford	1	Kidsgrove Athletic	2	
Qualifying 1	Stocksbridge Park Steels	3	Scarborough Athletic	4	
Qualifying 1	Stourbridge	3	Banbury United	2	
Qualifying 1	Swindon Supermarine	2	Bideford	3	
Qualifying 1	Thamesmead Town	1	Metropolitan Police	2	
Qualifying 1	Tiverton Town	3	Truro City	2	
Qualifying 1	Trafford	6	Wakefield	1	
Qualifying 1	Weymouth	1	Bridgwater Town	0	
Qualifying 1	Whitby Town	0	Chorley	1	
Qualifying 1	Whitstable Town	2	Potters Bar Town	2	
Qualifying 1	Wingate & Finchley	2	Hitchin Town	2	
Qualifying 1	Witham Town	0	St. Albans City	3	
Qualifying 1	Witton Albion	2	FC United of Manchester	2	
Qualifying 1	Wroxham	4	Margate	9	
Replay	Bedford Town	0	Hampton & Richmond Borough	2	
Replay	Burscough	0	Marine	1	
Replay	Darlington 1883	3	Buxton	3	(aet)
	Buxton won 4-3 on penalties				
Replay	East Thurrock United	6	Eastbourne Town	2	
Replay	Herne Bay	1	Grays Athletic	2	(aet)
Replay	Hitchin Town	0	Wingate & Finchley	1	
Replay	Kendal Town	1	AFC Fylde	2	
Replay	Poole Town	3	Frome Town	1	(aet)
Replay	Potters Bar Town	1	Whitstable Town	2	
Replay	Soham Town Rangers	4	Grantham Town	1	(aet)
Replay	Witton Albion	2	FC United of Manchester	1	
Qualifying 2	Arlesey Town	3	Poole Town	2	
Qualifying 2	Blyth Spartans	0	Ramsbottom United	1	
Qualifying 2	Bognor Regis Town	4	Chippenham Town	1	
Qualifying 2	Bury Town	2	Chatham Town	1	
Qualifying 2	Canvey Island	0	East Thurrock United	2	
Qualifying 2	Carshalton Athletic	2	Egham Town	1	
Qualifying 2	Chesham United	2	Weymouth	1	
Qualifying 2	Coalville Town	5	Marine	0	
Qualifying 2	Dulwich Hamlet	3	Leatherhead	0	
Qualifying 2	Enfield Town	0	Grays Athletic	1	
Qualifying 2	Folkestone Invicta	1	Hungerford Town	1	
Qualifying 2	Gresley	2	Trafford	0	
Qualifying 2	Hampton & Richmond Borough	2	Metropolitan Police	1	
Qualifying 2	Hastings United	0	AFC Sudbury	1	
Qualifying 2	Hemel Hempstead Town	9	North Greenford United	1	
Qualifying 2	Hendon	1	Bideford	0	
Qualifying 2	Hythe Town	2	Whitstable Town	2	
Qualifying 2	Kidsgrove Athletic	0	Curzon Ashton	4	
Qualifying 2	Margate	4	Clevedon Town	1	
Qualifying 2	Marlow	2	Burnham	0	
Qualifying 2	Matlock Town	2	St. Neots Town	0	
Qualifying 2	Merthyr Town	3	Dunstable Town	2	
Qualifying 2	Mickleover Sports	1	Stourbridge	2	
Qualifying 2	Northwich Victoria	2	Mossley	0	
Qualifying 2	Ramsgate	4	Three Bridges	1	
Qualifying 2	Redditch United	5	Brigg Town	0	
Qualifying 2	Rushall Olympic	0	AFC Fylde	1	

Qualifying 2	Scarborough Athletic	0	Cambridge City	0	
Qualifying 2	Sheffield	1	Buxton	0	
Qualifying 2	Soham Town Rangers	1	Chorley	2	
Qualifying 2	St. Albans City	3	Billericay Town	3	
Qualifying 2	St. Ives Town	1	Nantwich Town	4	
Qualifying 2	Tiverton Town	3	Mangotsfield United	1	
Qualifying 2	Wealdstone	2	Maidstone United	2	
Qualifying 2	Wingate & Finchley	1	Daventry Town	1	
Qualifying 2	Witton Albion	1	Leek Town	2	
Replay	Billericay Town	2	St. Albans City	2	(aet)
	St. Albans City won 4-2 on penalties				
Replay	Cambridge City	1	Scarborough Athletic	2	
Replay	Daventry Town	3	Wingate & Finchley	1	
Replay	Hungerford Town	1	Folkestone Invicta	1	(aet)
	Hungerford Town won 5-4 on penalties				
Replay	Maidstone United	1	Wealdstone	0	
Replay	Whitstable Town	2	Hythe Town	1	
Qualifying 3	AFC Telford United	6	Scarborough Athletic	0	
Qualifying 3	Arlesey Town	2	Marlow	0	
Qualifying 3	Barrow	2	Stockport County	2	
Qualifying 3	Basingstoke Town	3	Hampton & Richmond Borough	1	
Qualifying 3	Boreham Wood	0	Gloucester City	1	
Qualifying 3	Boston United	4	Redditch United	1	
Qualifying 3	Brackley Town	0	Leek Town	0	
Qualifying 3	Bury Town	5	Grays Athletic	1	
Qualifying 3	Carshalton Athletic	1	Whitstable Town	2	
Qualifying 3	Chelmsford City	1	St. Albans City	2	
Qualifying 3	Chorley	2	Matlock Town	0	
Qualifying 3	Colwyn Bay	0	Altrincham	2	
Qualifying 3	Curzon Ashton	2	AFC Fylde	1	
Qualifying 3	Daventry Town	3	Ramsgate	2	
Qualifying 3	Dover Athletic	1	Bath City	0	
Qualifying 3	Dulwich Hamlet	1	Concord Rangers	1	
Qualifying 3	East Thurrock United	4	Merthyr Town	2	
Qualifying 3	Eastbourne Borough	0	Maidenhead United	1	
Qualifying 3	Ebbsfleet United	4	Bromley	1	
Qualifying 3	Gosport Borough	3	Dorchester Town	0	
Qualifying 3	Guiseley	3	Histon	0	
Qualifying 3	Harrogate Town	1	Bradford Park Avenue	1	
Qualifying 3	Hayes & Yeading United	2	Bognor Regis Town	1	
Qualifying 3	Hednesford Town	3	Workington	0	
Qualifying 3	Hendon	2	Oxford City	1	
Qualifying 3	Hungerford Town	5	Hemel Hempstead Town	0	
Qualifying 3	Leamington	2	Gainsborough Trinity	0	
Qualifying 3	Maidstone United	1	Eastleigh	2	
Qualifying 3	Margate	0	Chesham United	3	
Qualifying 3	Northwich Victoria	2	Nantwich Town	0	
Qualifying 3	Sheffield	2	Gresley	4	
Qualifying 3	Solihull Moors	1	Coalville Town	2	
Qualifying 3	Staines Town	2	Farnborough	2	
Qualifying 3	Stalybridge Celtic	3	Vauxhall Motors	0	
Qualifying 3	Stourbridge	2	North Ferriby United	2	
Qualifying 3	Sutton United	1	Havant & Waterlooville	2	
Qualifying 3	Tonbridge Angels	1	AFC Sudbury	1	
Qualifying 3	Weston-Super-Mare	1	Tiverton Town	1	
Qualifying 3	Whitehawk	2	Bishop's Stortford	1	
Qualifying 3	Worcester City	3	Ramsbottom United	0	

Replay	AFC Sudbury	0	Tonbridge Angels	1	
Replay	Bradford Park Avenue	4	Harrogate Town	0	
Replay	Concord Rangers	4	Dulwich Hamlet	3	
Replay	Farnborough	0	Staines Town	2	
Replay	Leek Town	2	Brackley Town	1	(aet)
Replay	North Ferriby United	4	Stourbridge	0	
Replay	Stockport County	2	Barrow	3	
Replay	Tiverton Town	1	Weston-Super-Mare	2	
Round 1	Aldershot Town	1	Weston-Super-Mare	1	
Round 1	Alfreton Town	0	Nuneaton Town	1	
Round 1	Altrincham	1	Leek Town	2	
Round 1	Arlesey Town	1	Whitehawk	5	
Round 1	Basingstoke Town	0	Havant & Waterlooville	0	
Round 1	Bradford Park Avenue	2	Kidderminster Harriers	1	
Round 1	Braintree Town	3	Welling United	0	
Round 1	Bury Town	0	Eastleigh	3	
Round 1	Chester FC	1	Barrow	2	
Round 1	Chorley	2	Curzon Ashton	1	
Round 1	Coalville Town	1	Grimsby Town	1	
Round 1	Dartford	1	Forest Green Rovers	1	
Round 1	Daventry Town	0	Maidenhead United	1	
Round 1	East Thurrock United	1	Dover Athletic	1	
Round 1	Ebbsfleet United	3	Gloucester City	0	
Round 1	FC Halifax Town	0	Guiseley	1	
Round 1	Gateshead	4	Hednesford Town	1	
Round 1	Gosport Borough	1	Concord Rangers	0	
Round 1	Hayes & Yeading United	0	Barnet	1	
Round 1	Hendon	1	Whitstable Town	2	
Round 1	Hereford United	0	Woking	3	
Round 1	Hungerford Town	2	Chesham United	0	
Round 1	Hyde	1	North Ferriby United	2	
Round 1	Leamington	0	Northwich Victoria	0	
Round 1	Lincoln City	5	Stalybridge Celtic	1	
Round 1	Salisbury City	0	Cambridge United	1	
Round 1	Southport	1	Boston United	2	
Round 1	Staines Town	0	Luton Town	0	
Round 1	Tamworth	2	Macclesfield Town	0	
Round 1	Tonbridge Angels	0	St. Albans City	0	
Round 1	Worcester City	0	AFC Telford United	0	
Round 1	Wrexham	2	Gresley	1	
Replay	AFC Telford United	0	Worcester City	3	
Replay	Dover Athletic	3	East Thurrock United	1	
Replay	Forest Green Rovers	1	Dartford	0	
Replay	Grimsby Town	3	Coalville Town	0	
Replay	Havant & Waterlooville	1	Basingstoke Town	0	
Replay	Luton Town	2	Staines Town	0	
Replay	Northwich Victoria	0	Leamington	1	
Replay	St. Albans City	4	Tonbridge Angels	0	
Replay	Weston-Super-Mare	2	Aldershot Town	5	
Round 2	Aldershot Town	4	Worcester City	1	
Round 2	Barnet	1	Grimsby Town	2	
Round 2	Barrow	0	Maidenhead United	2	
Round 2	Braintree Town	1	Lincoln City	3	
Round 2	Chorley	0	Forest Green Rovers	0	
Round 2	Dover Athletic	2	Leamington	0	
Round 2	Eastleigh	2	Gateshead	0	

Round 2	Gosport Borough	0	Nuneaton Town	0	
Round 2	Guiseley	3	Bradford Park Avenue	0	
Round 2	Leek Town	0	Hungerford Town	1	
Round 2	Luton Town	2	Wrexham	0	
Round 2	North Ferriby United	4	Woking	0	
Round 2	St. Albans City	1	Cambridge United	2	
Round 2	Tamworth	2	Boston United	0	
Round 2	Whitehawk	1	Havant & Waterlooville	1	
Round 2	Whitstable Town	1	Ebbsfleet United	2	
Replay	Forest Green Rovers	0	Chorley	0	(aet)
	Chorley won 3-1 on penalties				
Replay	Havant & Waterlooville	3	Whitehawk	1	
Replay	Nuneaton Town	0	Gosport Borough	0	(aet)
	Gosport Borough won 4-2 on penalties				
Round 3	Aldershot Town	3	Guiseley	0	
Round 3	Cambridge United	2	Luton Town	2	
Round 3	Eastleigh	3	Dover Athletic	2	
Round 3	Grimsby Town	2	Maidenhead United	1	
Round 3	Havant & Waterlooville	1	Ebbsfleet United	0	
Round 3	Hungerford Town	0	Gosport Borough	1	
Round 3	Lincoln City	0	North Ferriby United	4	
Round 3	Tamworth	1	Chorley	1	
Replay	Chorley	2	Tamworth	2	(aet)
Replay	Luton Town	0	Cambridge United	1	
Round 4	Eastleigh	0	Cambridge United	1	
Round 4	Grimsby Town	4	Tamworth	1	
Round 4	Havant & Waterlooville	4	Aldershot Town	1	
Round 4	North Ferriby United	1	Gosport Borough	2	
Semi-finals					
1st leg	Cambridge United	2	Grimsby Town	1	
2nd leg	Grimsby Town	1	Cambridge United	1	
	Cambridge United won 3-2 on aggregate				
1st leg	Havant & Waterlooville	1	Gosport Borough	1	
2nd leg	Gosport Borough	2	Havant & Waterlooville	0	
	Gosport Borough won 4-1 on aggregate				
FINAL	Cambridge United	4	Gosport Borough	0	

F.A. Vase 2013/2014

Round 1	AFC Blackpool	1	Norton United	4	
Round 1	AFC Wulfrunians	5	Atherstone Town	0	
Round 1	Abingdon United	0	Fareham Town	3	(aet)
Round 1	Almondsbury UWE	2	Barnstaple Town	4	
Round 1	Alresford Town	4	Hythe & Dibden	1	
Round 1	Ashford United	4	Greenwich Borough	1	
Round 1	Baldock Town	1	Berkhamsted	4	
Round 1	Bartley Green	0	Alvechurch	6	
Round 1	Beckenham Town	4	Westfield	0	
Round 1	Billingham Synthonia	1	Guisborough Town	0	
Round 1	Binfield	9	Warminster Town	1	
Round 1	Blaby & Whetstone Athletic	5	Holbeach United	1	
Round 1	Bootle	4	Parkgate	5	
Round 1	Bovey Tracey	0	Shepton Mallet	2	
Round 1	Bradford Town	2	AFC Portchester	3	
Round 1	Bridlington Town	2	Sunderland RCA	0	
Round 1	Brightlingsea Regent	5	Team Bury	1	
Round 1	Brimscombe & Thrupp	3	Ashton & Backwell United	1	
Round 1	Brislington	1	Longwell Green Sports	0	
Round 1	Bishop Sutton	0	Odd Down	6	
Round 1	Buckland Athletic	4	Bristol Manor Farm	0	
Round 1	Cadbury Heath	1	Hallen	3	
Round 1	Chadderton	2	Athersley Recreation	3	
Round 1	Cheadle Town	1	Stockport Sports	0	
Round 1	Chessington & Hook United	3	Hassocks	0	
Round 1	Clapton	0	Barking	1	
Round 1	Cockfosters	3	Wembley	0	
Round 1	Coleshill Town	4	Racing Club Warwick	2	
Round 1	Cray Valley Paper Mills	2	AFC Croydon Athletic	0	
Round 1	Crowborough Athletic	1	Epsom Athletic	0	
Round 1	Diss Town	1	Eynesbury Rovers	3	
Round 1	Dorking	2	Knaphill	2	(aet)
Round 1	Dudley Town	7	Cradley Town	0	
Round 1	East Grinstead Town	2	Sevenoaks Town	0	
Round 1	Earlswood Town	0	Causeway United	1	
Round 1	Eastbourne United	5	Phoenix Sports	4	(aet)
Round 1	Erith Town	4	Lingfield	3	
Round 1	Farnham Town	0	East Preston	1	
Round 1	Garforth Town	1	Winsford United	2	(aet)
Round 1	Glossop North End	7	Kinsley Boys	0	
Round 1	Gorleston	0	Great Yarmouth Town	1	
Round 1	Graham Street Primitives	3	Harrowby United	1	
Round 1	Great Wakering Rovers	5	Ipswich Wanderers	2	
Round 1	Hamworthy United	1	Oxford City Nomads	2	
Round 1	Hanwell Town	4	London APSA	1	
Round 1	Harborough Town	0	Cleethorpes Town	5	
Round 1	Hartley Wintney	4	Petersfield Town	2	
Round 1	Heanor Town	4	Kirby Muxloe	2	(aet)
Round 1	Highmoor Ibis	2	Folland Sports	4	
Round 1	Hillingdon Borough	1	Hadley	2	(aet)
Round 1	Hucknall Town	1	Desborough Town	3	
Round 1	Huntingdon Town	3	Thetford Town	0	
Round 1	Ilford	2	Tring Athletic	3	
Round 1	Jarrow Roofing Boldon CA	2	Nelson	0	
Round 1	Kidlington	5	Lymington Town	1	

Round 1	Littlehampton Town	2	Corinthian	1	
Round 1	Liversedge	3	Armthorpe Welfare	4	
Round 1	Long Eaton United	2	Boston Town	0	
Round 1	Maine Road	3	Atherton LR	0	
Round 1	Moneyfields	1	Christchurch	1	(aet)
Round 1	North Shields	2	Crook Town	2	(aet)
Round 1	Newcastle Benfield	3	Marske United	2	
Round 1	Newhaven	4	Cove	4	(aet)
Round 1	Newmarket Town	1	Mildenhall Town	1	(aet)
Round 1	Norwich United	2	Bowers & Pitsea	1	(aet)
Round 1	Oxhey Jets	3	Stotfold	2	
Round 1	Pelsall Villa	0	Coventry Sphinx	2	
Round 1	Penrith	1	Morpeth Town	2	
Round 1	Plymouth Parkway	2	Gillingham Town	0	
Round 1	Radcliffe Olympic	2	Holwell Sports	3	(aet)
Round 1	Reading Town	2	Milton United (Oxon)	0	
Round 1	Retford United	0	Oadby Town	1	
Round 1	Rochdale Town	1	Congleton Town	3	
Round 1	Saltash United	2	Willand Rovers	1	
Round 1	Shawbury United	0	Bolehall Swifts	1	
Round 1	Sileby Rangers	2	AFC Mansfield	5	(aet)
Round 1	St. Andrews	4	Lincoln Moorlands Railway	0	
Round 1	St. Margaretsbury	0	Colney Heath	3	
Round 1	Staines Lammas	0	South Park	5	
Round 1	Staveley MW	2	West Didsbury & Chorlton	0	
Round 1	Stewarts & Lloyds	1	Loughborough University	2	
Round 1	Stourport Swifts	0	Brocton	2	
Round 1	Swaffham Town	2	Hullbridge Sports	2	(aet)
Round 1	Takeley	3	Sporting Bengal United	0	
Round 1	Tavistock	3	Winterbourne United	2	
Round 1	Thackley	1	Eccleshill United	0	
Round 1	Tower Hamlets	0	Haringey Borough	3	
Round 1	Verwood Town	3	Laverstock & Ford	1	
Round 1	West Auckland Town	5	South Shields	0	
Round 1	Walsham Le Willows	5	Godmanchester Rovers	0	
Round 1	Wantage Town	7	Abingdon Town	0	
Round 1	Welwyn Garden City	1	Barton Town Old Boys	0	
Round 1	Westfields	3	Bromsgrove Sporting	2	
Round 1	Whickham	1	Holker Old Boys	0	
Round 1	Whyteleafe	4	Windsor	2	
Round 1	Winchester City	0	Sholing	1	
Round 1	Woodford United	0	AFC Rushden & Diamonds	6	
Round 1	Worksop Parramore	3	Runcorn Linnets	1	
Replay	Christchurch	0	Moneyfields	1	
Replay	Cove	2	Newhaven	0	
Replay	Crook Town	4	North Shields	3	(aet)
Replay	Hullbridge Sports	4	Swaffham Town	3	(aet)
Replay	Knaphill	2	Dorking	1	
Replay	Mildenhall Town	0	Newmarket Town	2	(aet)
Round 2	AFC Emley	1	Jarrow Roofing Boldon CA	3	
Round 2	AFC Mansfield	1	Huntingdon Town	1	(aet)
Round 2	AFC Portchester	3	Shepton Mallet	1	
	Shepton Mallet progressed to Round 3 after AFC Portchester were expelled from the competition.				
Round 2	AFC Wulfrunians	2	AFC Rushden & Diamonds	4	(aet)
Round 2	Alvechurch	3	Oadby Town	0	
Round 2	Ampthill Town	7	Barking	0	

Round 2	Ascot United	0	Beckenham Town	1	
Round 2	Ashford United	1	Littlehampton Town	0	
Round 2	Ashington	3	Worksop Parramore	1	
Round 2	Athersley Recreation	0	Bridlington Town	1	(aet)
Round 2	Barnstaple Town	3	Hallen	4	
Round 2	Blaby & Whetstone Athletic	3	Desborough Town	0	
Round 2	Blackfield & Langley	1	Oxford City Nomads	0	
Round 2	Bodmin Town	4	Bemerton Heath Harlequins	2	
Round 2	Bolehall Swifts	–	Heanor Town	–	

Heanor Town were expelled from the competition. Walkover for Bolehall Swifts

Round 2	Borrowash Victoria	1	Congleton Town	4	
Round 2	Brimscombe & Thrupp	0	Binfield	3	
Round 2	Buckland Athletic	0	Saltash United	3	
Round 2	Causeway United	4	Dudley Town	1	
Round 2	Chessington & Hook United	2	Eastbourne United	3	
Round 2	Cleethorpes Town	1	Morpeth Town	6	
Round 2	Colney Heath	2	Newmarket Town	1	
Round 2	Dunston UTS	2	Crook Town	1	
Round 2	Ely City	0	Welwyn Garden City	0	(aet)
Round 2	Enfield 1893	2	Norwich United	3	
Round 2	Erith Town	5	Hartley Wintney	1	
Round 2	Fareham Town	0	Bitton	3	
Round 2	Folland Sports	1	Sholing	2	
Round 2	Gornal Athletic	3	Wisbech Town	6	(aet)
Round 2	Graham Street Primitives	3	Loughborough University	2	(aet)
Round 2	Great Wakering Rovers	2	Cockfosters	0	
Round 2	Great Yarmouth Town	1	Hanwell Town	2	
Round 2	Hadley	1	Brantham Athletic	2	
Round 2	Hanworth Villa	3	East Grinstead Town	1	
Round 2	Holwell Sports	2	Rocester	1	(aet)
Round 2	Hullbridge Sports	1	Berkhamsted	0	(aet)
Round 2	Kidlington	3	Tavistock	0	
Round 2	Knaphill	0	East Preston	4	
Round 2	Larkhall Athletic	2	Newport (IOW)	0	
Round 2	Long Eaton United	0	Coleshill Town	2	(aet)
Round 2	Lordswood	2	Whyteleafe	1	
Round 2	Maine Road	2	Billingham Synthonia	3	
Round 2	Newcastle Benfield	6	Cheadle Town	2	
Round 2	Norton United	0	Brighouse Town	2	
Round 2	Odd Down	2	Moneyfields	3	
Round 2	Oxhey Jets	2	Hadleigh United	3	
Round 2	Plymouth Parkway	3	Wantage Town	0	
Round 2	Reading Town	1	Brislington	0	
Round 2	Rye United	3	Cove	0	
Round 2	South Park	1	Cray Valley Paper Mills	1	(aet)
Round 2	Spennymoor Town	7	Winsford United	0	
Round 2	St. Andrews	2	Brocton	1	
Round 2	Staveley MW	2	Glossop North End	0	
Round 2	Takeley	1	Brightlingsea Regent	2	
Round 2	Thackley	4	Armthorpe Welfare	0	
Round 2	Tring Athletic	1	Eynesbury Rovers	0	
Round 2	Tunbridge Wells	1	Crowborough Athletic	0	
Round 2	Verwood Town	1	Alresford Town	4	
Round 2	West Auckland Town	1	Shildon	0	
Round 2	Walsall Wood	0	Spalding United	3	

Spalding Town were subsequently expelled from the competition. Walkover for Walsall Wood.

Round 2	Walsham Le Willows	1	Haringey Borough	4	

Round 2	Westfields	6	Coventry Sphinx	1	
Round 2	Whickham	3	Parkgate	0	
Round 2	Whitley Bay	3	Runcorn Town	0	
Round 2	Winsford United	0	Spennymoor Town	0	(aet)
Replay	Cray Valley Paper Mills	2	South Park	3	
Replay	Huntingdon Town	1	AFC Mansfield	0	
Replay	Welwyn Garden City	3	Ely City	0	
Round 3	AFC Rushden & Diamonds	2	Graham Street Primitives	0	
Round 3	Alvechurch	0	Westfields	1	
Round 3	Ampthill Town	2	Beckenham Town	1	
Round 3	Ashford United	1	Tring Athletic	0	
Round 3	Ashington	1	Thackley	0	
Round 3	Binfield	0	Larkhall Athletic	1	
Round 3	Blaby & Whetstone Athletic	1	Causeway United	2	
Round 3	Brighouse Town	3	Whickham	3	(aet)
Round 3	Brightlingsea Regent	2	Colney Heath	2	(aet)
Round 3	Congleton Town	2	Huntingdon Town	1	
Round 3	East Preston	2	Rye United	1	
Round 3	Great Wakering Rovers	0	Hullbridge Sports	1	
Round 3	Hadleigh United	3	Welwyn Garden City	2	(aet)
Round 3	Hanwell Town	5	Lordswood	0	
Round 3	Haringey Borough	2	Brantham Athletic	3	(aet)
Round 3	Holwell Sports	1	Coleshill Town	3	
Round 3	Jarrow Roofing Boldon CA	1	Newcastle Benfield	2	
Round 3	Kidlington	2	Bodmin Town	3	(aet)
Round 3	Moneyfields	–	Bitton	–	
	Both teams were expelled from the competition after the game was abandoned due to a mass brawl.				
Round 3	Norwich United	3	Erith Town	0	
Round 3	Plymouth Parkway	1	Hallen	3	
Round 3	Reading Town	1	Sholing	4	
Round 3	Saltash United	2	Alresford Town	7	
Round 3	Shepton Mallet	2	Blackfield & Langley	2	
Round 3	South Park	1	Eastbourne United	2	
Round 3	Spennymoor Town	2	Bridlington Town	0	
Round 3	St. Andrews	4	Bolehall Swifts	1	
Round 3	Staveley MW	0	Morpeth Town	2	
Round 3	Tunbridge Wells	0	Hanworth Villa	1	
Round 3	West Auckland Town	2	Billingham Synthonia	1	
Round 3	Walsall Wood	0	Wisbech Town	1	
Round 3	Whitley Bay	0	Dunston UTS	2	
Replay	Colney Heath	0	Brightlingsea Regent	2	
Replay	Whickham	1	Brighouse Town	0	
Round 4	AFC Rushden & Diamonds	0	St. Andrews	2	
Round 4	Ampthill Town	3	Norwich United	1	
Round 4	Ashford United	1	Hanwell Town	2	
Round 4	Ashington	1	Wisbech Town	2	
Round 4	Brightlingsea Regent	3	Bodmin Town	1	
Round 4	Dunston UTS	2	Coleshill Town	1	(aet)
Round 4	East Preston	3	Brantham Athletic	0	N
Round 4	Hadleigh United received a bye after Moneyfields and Bitton were both expelled from the competition.				
Round 4	Hallen	2	Alresford Town	0	
Round 4	Hanworth Villa	2	Eastbourne United	7	(aet)
Round 4	Larkhall Athletic	3	Blackfield & Langley	0	
Round 4	Morpeth Town	3	Westfields	0	
Round 4	Newcastle Benfield	3	Congleton Town	1	

Round 4	Sholing	3	Hullbridge Sports	1	
Round 4	Spennymoor Town	1	Causeway United	0	
Round 4	Whickham	1	West Auckland Town	3	(aet)
Round 5	Ampthill Town	3	Hanwell Town	1	(aet)
Round 5	Dunston UTS	5	Brightlingsea Regent	0	
Round 5	East Preston	1	St. Andrews	2	
Round 5	Eastbourne United	6	Morpeth Town	1	
Round 5	Hadleigh United	1	Wisbech Town	2	
Round 5	Sholing	1	Larkhall Athletic	0	(aet)
Round 5	Spennymoor Town	1	Newcastle Benfield	2	
Round 5	West Auckland Town	2	Hallen	0	
Round 6	Dunston UTS	0	West Auckland Town	1	
Round 6	Eastbourne United	2	Ampthill Town	1	
Round 6	Sholing	1	Wisbech Town	0	
Round 6	St. Andrews	1	Newcastle Benfield	0	

Semi-finals

1st leg	Sholing	2	Eastbourne United	0	
2nd leg	Eastbourne United	2	Sholing	4	
	Sholing won 6-2 on aggregate.				
1st leg	West Auckland Town	0	St. Andrews	0	
2nd leg	St. Andrews	1	West Auckland Town	2	
	West Auckland Town won 2-1 on aggregate.				
FINAL	Sholing	1	West Auckland Town	0	

Football Conference National Fixtures 2014/2015 Season	AFC Telford United	Aldershot Town	Alfreton Town	Altrincham	Barnet	Braintree Town	Bristol Rovers	Chester	Dartford	Dover Athletic	Eastleigh	Forest Green Rovers	Gateshead	Grimsby Town	FC Halifax Town	Kidderminster Harriers	Lincoln City	Macclesfield Town	Nuneaton Town	Southport	Torquay United	Welling United	Woking	Wrexham
AFC Telford United		16/08	28/02	11/11	13/09	22/11	01/11	30/09	14/02	06/09	20/12	07/10	28/12	29/11	24/01	04/04	11/04	12/08	01/01	25/08	27/09	09/12	14/03	25/04
Aldershot Town	04/01		04/10	09/08	26/12	16/09	11/10	18/04	28/02	24/01	22/11	23/08	01/11	30/08	07/02	06/12	20/09	09/12	15/11	14/03	06/04	14/02	09/09	28/03
Alfreton Town	16/09	21/02		09/09	28/03	30/08	11/11	21/03	28/12	15/11	09/12	24/01	02/12	06/04	30/09	07/03	01/01	20/12	20/09	07/02	11/10	18/04	09/08	23/08
Altrincham	18/04	31/01	01/11		28/02	18/10	16/08	01/01	06/09	20/12	13/09	14/02	25/08	15/11	21/03	29/11	12/08	30/09	28/12	04/04	17/01	27/09	11/10	14/03
Barnet	15/11	01/01	06/09	20/09		21/10	12/08	20/12	25/08	28/12	04/10	07/03	25/04	21/02	11/04	11/10	16/08	29/11	04/04	24/01	11/11	21/03	07/02	16/09
Braintree Town	21/03	11/04	14/02	25/04	30/09		06/09	16/08	01/01	12/08	28/12	17/01	07/03	04/11	27/09	13/09	04/04	31/01	25/08	11/10	20/12	25/11	01/11	15/11
Bristol Rovers	23/08	21/03	25/04	21/02	25/11	24/01		04/04	07/10	04/10	07/03	18/10	20/12	09/08	30/08	15/11	07/02	28/12	16/09	11/04	01/01	29/11	20/09	09/09
Chester	02/12	07/10	18/10	26/12	09/08	04/01	22/11		07/02	11/04	21/02	06/04	15/11	14/03	23/08	24/01	06/12	06/09	25/04	16/09	09/09	04/10	28/03	20/09
Dartford	30/08	18/10	14/03	28/03	06/04	26/12	31/01	25/11		16/09	09/09	20/09	21/02	04/10	06/12	04/01	25/04	11/10	11/04	15/11	23/08	11/11	24/01	09/08
Dover	28/03	14/03	27/09	07/02	09/09	11/11	18/04	11/10	17/01		23/08	22/11	21/03	04/01	09/08	30/08	07/03	13/09	25/11	21/02	02/12	26/12	06/04	06/12
Eastleigh	07/02	12/08	11/04	04/01	14/03	20/09	30/09	01/11	02/12	04/04		16/09	16/08	06/12	11/11	25/04	15/11	28/02	18/10	06/09	14/02	25/08	26/12	24/01
Forest Green Rovers	21/02	06/09	16/08	06/12	27/09	14/03	25/08	12/08	29/11	25/04	01/11		11/10	07/02	13/09	26/12	01/11	11/04	31/01	28/02	30/09	04/01	09/12	06/09
Gateshead	09/09	27/09	07/10	06/04	18/10	04/10	28/02	30/08	13/09	29/11	28/03	18/04		23/08	26/12	07/02	11/11	14/03	14/02	09/12	09/08	24/01	06/12	04/01
Grimsby Town	31/01	25/04	25/08	07/10	17/01	28/02	14/02	27/09	01/11	16/08	21/03	20/12	04/04		11/11	22/11	28/12	01/01	12/08	30/09	13/09	06/09	25/11	11/04
FC Halifax Town	20/09	06/09	29/11	04/10	31/01	21/02	14/03	28/12	07/03	14/02	17/01	02/12	01/01	16/09		18/10	25/08	04/04	20/12	12/08	18/04	16/08	15/11	07/10
Kidderminster Harr.	04/10	11/11	12/08	16/09	18/04	28/03	06/04	25/08	16/08	14/03	31/01	01/01	06/09	20/09	28/02		20/12	17/01	02/12	28/12	01/11	07/10	14/02	25/11
Lincoln City	11/10	17/01	26/12	04/11	04/01	23/08	13/09	14/02	22/11	31/01	18/04	28/03	30/09	09/09	06/04	09/08		27/09	09/12	29/11	30/08	14/03	28/02	18/10
Macclesfield Town	06/12	07/03	22/11	24/01	07/10	09/08	28/03	11/11	18/04	18/10	30/08	04/10	16/09	26/12	09/09	23/08	21/02		21/03	20/09	25/11	07/02	04/01	06/04
Nuneaton Town	26/12	13/09	06/12	30/08	23/08	06/04	04/01	29/11	27/09	07/10	09/08	09/09	17/01	24/01	28/03	21/02	04/10	01/11		22/11	14/03	28/02	18/04	07/02
Southport	06/04	25/11	13/09	23/08	30/08	06/12	27/09	17/01	21/03	01/11	10/02	09/08	31/01	18/04	04/01	09/09	07/10	14/02	07/03		28/03	18/10	04/10	26/12
Torquay United	07/03	25/08	04/01	11/04	06/12	07/02	26/12	28/02	04/04	20/09	29/11	15/11	22/11	18/10	09/12	21/03	24/01	25/04	06/09	16/08		12/08	16/09	04/10
Welling United	09/08	20/12	17/01	07/03	01/11	09/09	06/12	31/01	30/09	01/01	06/04	30/08	20/09	28/03	22/11	11/04	16/09	15/11	11/10	25/04	28/12		23/08	21/12
Woking	18/10	28/12	31/01	02/12	22/11	29/11	17/01	13/09	12/08	25/08	01/01	21/03	11/04	07/03	25/04	27/09	06/09	16/08	30/09	20/12	21/02	21/02		11/11
Wrexham	17/01	29/11	04/04	22/11	14/02	18/04	02/12	07/03	20/12	28/02	27/09	28/12	12/08	11/10	01/11	30/09	21/03	25/08	16/08	01/01	31/01	13/09	30/08	

Please note that the above fixtures may be subject to change.

Football Conference North Fixtures 2014/2015 Season	AFC Fylde	Barrow	Boston United	Brackley Town	Bradford Park Avenue	Chorley	Colwyn Bay	Gainsborough Trinity	Gloucester City	Guiseley	Harrogate Town	Hednesford Town	Hyde	Leamington	Lowestoft Town	North Ferriby United	Oxford City	Solihull Moors	Stalybridge Celtic	Stockport County	Tamworth	Worcester City
AFC Fylde	■	26/12	10/01	09/08	09/09	31/01	06/04	18/10	25/04	23/08	14/02	30/08	21/03	08/11	04/01	04/10	17/01	11/04	06/12	22/11	28/02	20/09
Barrow	01/01	■	20/12	31/01	28/03	25/08	17/01	12/08	18/10	01/11	28/12	13/01	16/08	13/09	04/10	28/02	14/03	14/02	15/11	04/04	18/04	06/09
Boston United	01/11	09/08	■	06/12	14/02	15/11	04/01	21/03	20/09	24/01	28/02	04/10	18/10	25/04	26/12	23/08	09/09	02/12	30/08	31/01	06/04	28/03
Brackley Town	20/12	11/04	12/08	■	22/11	07/03	01/11	16/08	01/01	06/09	10/01	25/04	13/09	28/12	24/01	21/03	07/02	04/04	04/10	28/02	18/10	25/08
Bradford Park Ave.	04/04	06/10	06/09	20/09	■	01/01	24/01	07/02	20/12	11/04	11/08	28/02	25/08	16/08	21/02	25/10	13/01	15/11	14/03	28/12	01/11	18/04
Chorley	14/03	06/04	08/11	30/08	26/12	■	06/12	24/01	14/02	07/02	04/10	20/09	22/11	25/10	09/08	09/09	04/01	25/04	23/08	11/11	28/03	28/02
Colwyn Bay	25/08	25/10	16/08	28/03	08/11	12/08	■	06/09	22/11	04/04	25/11	31/01	28/12	28/02	18/04	13/09	04/10	20/12	10/01	01/01	14/03	14/02
Gainsborough Trinity	28/03	06/12	25/10	04/01	30/08	01/11	15/11	■	06/04	11/11	31/01	09/08	28/02	14/03	23/08	26/12	18/04	21/02	20/09	17/01	09/09	04/10
Gloucester City	13/09	13/12	14/03	26/12	09/08	11/04	21/02	10/01	■	15/11	08/11	23/08	06/09	04/04	31/01	04/01	01/03	07/10	25/10	18/04	06/12	18/01
Guiseley	28/12	22/11	21/02	14/03	17/01	18/04	09/09	25/08	30/08	■	01/01	14/02	31/01	20/12	08/11	28/03	20/09	25/10	06/04	12/08	04/10	16/08
Harrogate Town	18/04	23/08	17/01	25/10	06/12	21/02	21/03	07/10	07/03	26/12	■	04/01	15/11	07/02	28/03	06/04	30/08	13/09	09/09	01/11	09/08	22/11
Hednesford Town	07/02	08/11	07/03	21/02	18/10	17/01	07/10	20/12	28/12	13/09	16/08	■	04/04	12/08	10/01	14/03	28/03	25/08	18/04	06/09	22/11	01/01
Hyde	21/02	04/01	07/02	18/04	06/04	06/10	23/08	08/11	24/01	07/03	14/03	08/09	■	01/12	20/09	06/12	09/08	10/01	26/12	28/03	30/08	25/10
Leamington	07/03	21/02	22/11	23/08	04/01	10/01	30/08	14/02	09/09	09/08	20/09	06/12	04/10	■	06/04	18/04	26/12	31/01	28/03	18/10	17/01	01/11
Lowestoft Town	16/08	25/04	01/01	07/10	13/09	20/12	07/02	28/12	01/11	21/03	06/09	11/04	17/01	25/08	■	22/11	18/10	12/08	28/02	14/03	15/11	04/04
North Ferriby United	15/11	20/09	28/12	13/01	25/04	04/04	11/04	01/01	16/08	18/10	25/08	24/01	12/08	06/10	07/03	■	01/11	06/09	21/02	20/12	14/02	31/01
Oxford City	06/09	24/01	04/04	15/11	21/03	16/08	07/03	13/09	25/08	25/04	11/04	25/10	20/12	01/01	14/02	10/01	■	28/12	08/11	07/10	31/01	12/08
Solihull Moors	13/01	30/08	18/04	17/01	04/10	18/10	09/08	22/11	28/03	28/02	24/01	06/04	01/11	21/03	06/12	07/02	23/08	■	04/01	20/09	26/12	14/03
Stalybridge Celtic	12/08	07/03	11/04	14/02	31/01	28/12	18/10	25/04	21/03	07/10	04/04	01/11	01/01	06/09	11/11	17/01	22/11	16/08	■	25/08	13/09	20/12
Stockport County	25/10	10/01	13/09	08/11	23/08	21/03	26/12	11/04	04/10	06/12	25/04	15/11	14/02	24/01	30/08	09/08	06/04	07/03	07/02	■	04/01	16/09
Tamworth	07/10	07/02	25/08	25/11	07/03	06/09	20/09	04/04	12/08	10/01	20/12	21/03	25/04	11/04	25/10	08/11	21/02	01/01	24/01	16/08	■	28/12
Worcester City	24/01	21/03	30/09	07/04	10/01	13/09	25/04	07/03	07/02	04/01	18/10	26/12	11/04	15/11	09/09	30/08	06/12	08/11	09/08	21/02	23/08	■

Please note that the above fixtures may be subject to change.

Football Conference South Fixtures 2014/2015 Season	Basingstoke Town	Bath City	Bishop's Stortford	Boreham Wood	Bromley	Chelmsford City	Concord Rangers	Eastbourne Borough	Ebbsfleet United	Farnborough	Gosport Borough	Havant & Waterlooville	Hayes & Yeading United	Hemel Hempstead Town	Maidenhead United	St. Albans City	Staines Town	Sutton United	Wealdstone	Weston-super-Mare	Whitehawk
Basingstoke Town		24/01	21/02	20/09	25/10	01/11	28/02	04/01	30/08	06/04	17/01	18/04	23/08	09/08	07/02	15/11	26/12	06/12	28/03	02/12	07/10
Bath City	12/08		07/02	28/12	28/03	16/08	14/03	20/09	21/02	02/12	07/10	25/08	28/02	25/10	15/11	01/11	17/01	18/04	20/12	01/01	06/09
Bishop's Stortford	06/09	13/09		01/01	07/10	25/08	20/12	15/11	14/02	28/03	18/04	28/12	10/01	01/11	16/08	04/04	31/01	14/03	12/08	28/02	20/09
Boreham Wood	31/01	30/08	26/12		23/08	13/09	14/02	08/09	04/01	09/08	22/11	28/02	06/12	28/03	10/11	06/10	18/04	06/04	08/11	25/10	14/03
Bromley	16/08	18/10	08/11	04/04		06/09	01/01	11/04	07/03	10/01	20/09	31/01	14/02	11/15	25/08	20/12	21/03	22/11	28/12	18/04	12/08
Chelmsford City	07/03	22/11	06/04	25/04	28/02		06/10	12/01	26/12	04/01	09/08	28/03	24/01	06/12	21/03	07/02	30/08	23/08	25/10	20/09	31/01
Concord Rangers	04/10	09/08	09/09	15/11	26/12	02/12		23/08	28/03	06/12	30/08	10/01	18/04	06/04	18/10	07/03	04/01	07/02	13/09	01/11	24/01
Eastbourne Borough	10/01	31/01	21/03	20/12	01/11	12/08	04/04		22/11	18/04	07/03	14/02	25/10	13/09	28/12	25/08	04/10	28/03	24/01	16/08	01/01
Ebbsfleet United	28/12	08/11	25/04	11/04	24/01	01/01	12/08	07/10		15/11	25/10	16/08	28/10	28/02	14/03	06/09	10/01	20/09	25/08	20/12	04/04
Farnborough	25/08	21/03	11/11	24/01	13/09	11/04	25/04	21/02	04/10		01/11	06/09	22/11	14/02	20/12	16/08	07/03	18/10	04/04	12/08	28/12
Gosport Borough	20/12	14/02	24/01	06/09	25/04	14/03	28/12	18/10	31/01	28/02		01/01	08/11	04/10	19/08	11/04	15/11	10/01	16/08	04/04	13/09
Havant & Waterloo.	13/09	06/04	30/08	04/10	09/08	18/10	08/11	06/12	21/03	07/02	26/12		04/01	09/09	21/02	13/01	23/08	24/01	14/03	15/11	28/04
Hayes & Yeading Utd	04/04	11/04	04/10	18/10	15/11	20/12	16/08	07/02	13/09	14/03	27/01	18/01		21/03	01/01	25/04	21/02	02/11	06/09	28/12	25/08
Hemel Hempstead T.	22/11	07/03	11/04	12/08	14/03	21/02	25/08	25/04	18/10	17/01	07/02	20/12	20/09		04/04	01/01	08/11	27/01	10/01	06/09	16/08
Maidenhead United	08/11	04/01	17/01	07/03	06/04	14/02	31/01	30/08	06/12	09/09	28/03	20/09	26/12	23/08		24/01	25/10	09/08	18/04	07/10	28/02
St. Albans City	14/02	06/12	23/08	10/01	08/09	04/10	17/01	06/04	18/04	25/10	04/01	22/11	09/08	26/12	13/09		28/03	30/08	28/02	14/03	08/11
Staines Town	01/01	25/04	22/11	16/08	07/02	28/12	11/04	14/03	01/11	20/09	13/01	04/04	07/10	24/01	06/09	12/08		28/02	14/02	20/08	18/10
Sutton United	11/04	04/10	25/10	25/08	21/02	04/04	06/09	08/11	17/01	31/01	21/03	12/08	07/03	15/11	25/04	28/12	13/09		01/01	14/02	20/12
Wealdstone	18/10	08/09	07/03	21/03	30/08	17/01	22/11	09/08	06/04	23/08	21/02	06/10	31/01	04/01	01/11	20/09	06/12	26/12		07/02	11/04
Weston-super-Mare	25/04	26/12	09/08	21/02	06/12	10/01	21/03	17/01	09/09	08/11	23/08	07/03	30/08	31/01	11/04	18/10	06/04	04/01	04/10		22/11
Whitehawk	21/03	10/01	04/01	07/02	17/01	15/11	25/10	26/12	23/08	30/08	06/12	01/11	06/04	18/04	04/10	21/02	09/08	09/09	16/09	28/03	

Please note that the above fixtures may be subject to change.